CRITICISM—OPPORTUNITY!

How do you react when someone hurls a string of critical, painful words at you? When a sharp comment cuts into your self-confidence? Do you feel hurt? Angry? Powerless?

Criticism doesn't have to be a liability! It can be a tremendous opportunity for personal and professional growth.

By simply changing the way you think about criticism, you can learn new responses that will enable you to maintain control. There are simple, effective ways to minimize the negative effects of criticism and open yourself to its benefits.

And that's what this book is all about. . . .

WHEN
WORDS
HURT

*How To Keep Criticism
from Undermining Your
Self-Esteem*

Mary Lynne Heldmann

BALLANTINE BOOKS • NEW YORK

Library of Congress Catalog Card Number: 87-63447

ISBN 0-345-35893-7

This edition published by arrangement with New Chapter Press, Inc.

Manufactured in the United States of America

First Ballantine Books Edition: January 1990

To Mom and Dad
Evelyn and Walter Heldmann
for giving me love, a sense of security, and room to grow

Contents

Acknowledgments

THERE ARE SEVERAL people I would like to salute and to whom I wish to express my deep gratitude for their contribution to my work over the years.

First and foremost, my three sons, Patrick, David, and Mark Cunningham, who have not only been a source of complete joy from the moment they poked their little heads into this world, but have unknowingly been a significant inspiration as well. For years I have watched them observe, assimilate, and then use many of the skills described in this book in many and varied situations.

My parents and my siblings and their spouses have been most helpful, loving, and supportive. A special thanks to my sister Phyllis Georges for helping me with some of my research.

I especially wish to thank my husband, Ben Patrick, for his ongoing efforts in adjusting to life with someone who wishes she had more hours in the day to do all she wants to do. Not only does he share time with kids, career, exercise program, friends, and dog, but recently he has had to accommodate my word processor as well.

There are a number of professionals and colleagues who have generously given their time, knowledge, and experience: the psychoanalyst Dr. Alberta Szalita, New York; David Crocker of IBM, New York; Marshall Goldsmith, Tony Reilly, John Garbarino, and Judy Bardwick of Keilty, Goldsmith, and Boone, La Jolla, California; Frank Wagner of Prism Consultants Ltd., Santa Monica, California; Steve Smoller of the Mental Health Center, Glens Falls Hospital, Glens Falls, New York; Pat Lamb, marriage and family counselor, Glens Falls, New York; John Mann, of Manndate Inc., New York; Josh Patrick of Patrick's Food Service, Burlington, Vermont; Jim Fahey of IBM, Poughkeepsie.

The Rev. Alfred Ashline, my friend and neighbor for more than fifteen years, fanned my ideas as they sparked and was always available to discuss, probe, and ponder. I appreciate not only his intellect but his support and encouragement.

Alice Dunkley, my right hand, kept the home office on keel while I dashed around the country and to my boys' soccer games.

Bob Dines of IBM, White Plains, first opened that corporate giant's door to me ten years ago. Bob has continued to offer his guidance and support over the years.

Bob Cadwallader of IBM, Poughkeepsie, expressed so much faith in me and my work when I needed it most.

Florence Cohn of Honigsbaum's Inc., Glens Falls, New York, and Nancy Patrick of Nan Patrick's, Burlington, Vermont, saved me hundreds of shopping hours by acting as my fashion consultants.

The thousands of workshop participants, as well as individual clients, whose straightforwardness and endless desire to learn and grow have been a great inspiration and learning tool for me.

For their help in the preparation of this manuscript, my deepest gratitude is extended to:

Wendy Crisp, publisher of New Chapter Press, who suggested this project in the first place and then offered her enthusiastic support throughout.

My dear friends Chris Shaw and Gary McGlouth, two talented writers, who both helped me get started and were always there when I needed a little encouragement.

They have continued to express their belief in me and what I have to say in other writing projects as well.

Mary Jo Territo, editor and miracle worker, who very quickly and efficiently cut my oversized manuscript without deleting a single critical point.

Kathryn Arnold and Mary Tooley, two tireless workhorses at New Chapter Press.

Sandra McCabe, friend and typist, astounded me as she deftly transcribed the first draft from my audio tapes.

The folks at Foothills Computer, Glens Falls, New York: Dr. Jeff, Brian, and Connie. They exemplify quality customer service par excellence, and they were always there when I needed them.

The more than a hundred men and women who so generously donated their time for my interviews.

I would like to offer a very special thank you to my wonderful friends who have given me so much support as I have attempted to maintain a balance between professional and personal endeavors.

Introduction

Sticks and stones may break my bones,
But words will never hurt me.

EVERY CHILD WHO has ever been called stupid or ugly or fat or clumsy knows that words *do* hurt. But somehow, like a parent's kiss on a skinned knee, repeating this age-old formula helps take away some of the sting of hurtful words. Shouting the familiar rhyme back at a bully or a know-it-all can help restore a child's self-esteem, or even instill a sense of moral superiority over the critic.

But what happens when someone hurls a string of critical, painful words at an adult? Although we do not respond to our attacker with a scrap of schoolyard doggerel, more often than not we act like children. We get defensive, deny responsibility, strike back, or withdraw in silence to seethe or plot revenge. Not only are these responses ineffective, they prevent us from using criticism as it should be used—as an aid to learning and growth.

Over the past ten years, in my work as a management consultant and workshop leader, I have seen the destructive effects that criticism can have in the workplace: the hourly worker who stammers, sweats, and turns crimson when asked to improve performance, the high-level executive who is locked into a ridiculous position because of a hot-headed response to a colleague's remark.

The effects of poorly delivered or poorly taken criticism are no less serious at home: the wife who snipes at her husband in front of others because she's not getting her way, the husband who hides behind his newspaper when criticized for not doing his share of the household chores.

All over the country, in every group I've worked with —governmental agencies, Fortune 500 companies, small and medium-sized businesses, banks, hospitals, school districts, community organizations—I have observed the same habitual responses to criticism. No matter where or who, people set up the same roadblocks to good communication and feedback. Individuals lose self-esteem, intimate relationships flounder, organizations become inefficient and unwieldy.

But it doesn't have to be that way. There are simple, effective ways to minimize the negative effects of criticism and become open to its benefits. There are simple, effective ways to give tactful, helpful criticism. And that's what this book is about.

The information in this book was developed from data I collected from thousands of workshop participants, from interviews with more than a hundred men and women from various walks of life, from working relationships with scores of human resources development specialists, and from my studies of pertinent psychological literature and the work of other management consultants.

This book will teach you to understand your habitual, childish responses to criticism and why they undermine your self-esteem; understand your thoughts and feelings about criticism; listen and think objectively about the criticism you receive; analyze your critic's intent; take control of your responses to criticism; cope with criticism by using a number of carefully formulated techniques; give constructive criticism.

If I taught a workshop every day for the next fifty years, I still would not be able to reach all the people I believe can benefit from my training program. I hope this book will help those I cannot work with personally to learn the skills that have been so useful to so many workshop participants.

Criticism is probably the most undervalued and least understood tool for human communication. Learning—and using—the techniques in this book will give you the opportunity to turn criticism into an asset instead of a liability. They will enable you to leave behind your impulse to respond to criticism with childish behavior because you will know that words don't have to hurt.

Mary Lynne Heldmann
Glens Falls, New York
March 1988

PART ONE

When Words Hurt

1

How and Why Criticism Undermines Your Self-Esteem

LAURA IS THE head night nurse in the intensive-care unit of a large hospital. The shift has been long and eventful, and Laura is making her final entries in patients' charts before turning the ward over to the day nurse.

Dr. Meade sweeps angrily into the nurses' station and thrusts a chart under her nose. "You woke me up in the middle of the night. Why?" he demands.

Laura quickly looks for the name at the top of the chart. "That's Ms. Murray's patient. She called you."

"You're in charge here; you authorized the call and I'm holding you responsible."

Laura flushes. "I was told the patient's vital signs—"

"You were told!" Dr. Meade interrupts. "Don't you supervise your nurses? Isn't that your job?"

Laura's color deepens; she feels her heart begin to pound. "I can't check on every single thing every single nurse does. I just don't have the time. Ms. Murray's description of the patient's condition seemed to indicate you should be called."

"Well, I shouldn't have been. What do you think I am? A machine? I need some sleep, too."

Surreptitiously Laura wipes her sweaty palms on her uniform. "Dr. Meade, three days ago you were angry

3

because I didn't authorize a call. You told me then to use my judgment and call you whenever—"

"*Judgment*! You haven't the judgment of a five-year-old!"

Dr. Meade stalks off, leaving Laura feeling childish, confused and belittled. She looks around, hoping no one has witnessed the demeaning scene. *I'm going to steer clear of him*, she promises herself. As she turns back to her work, her hands are still shaking.

Laura's reaction to the doctor's criticism is not unusual. We often respond defensively and feel uncomfortable when criticized. Our degree of discomfort depends on many variables: who our critic is; the intent of the critic; the way in which the criticism is delivered; the circumstances that occasioned the criticism; our state of mind. However, everyone has experienced some degree of real physiological and psychological discomfort when criticized.

The question is, why?

CRITICISM = DANGER

We may not be battling saber-toothed tigers for survival these days, but there are plenty of other dangers around. Remember the last time you stepped off a curb without checking for traffic? Remember the way you jumped back at the sound of the horn, the way your heart rate speeded up, the way your breathing became short and shallow? Your physiological response served you well, as it has for eons in preserving the species.

Much of the danger in our everyday modern lives comes not from the physical world, but from the behavior of other people. A reprimand, an argument, a rejection, a cutting comment elicits the same physiological response as a saber-toothed tiger once did or a speeding car does now.

Why does criticism so often seem like a threat? Think

back to when you were a child. What followed criticism? Punishment. Or unpleasant thoughts and feelings such as guilt, anxiety, hurt, isolation. Those thoughts and feelings became so much a part of criticism when we were growing up that now we experience them at even the first hint of criticism. Notice your response the next time you hear someone say in a serious tone: *There's something I want to talk to you about . . .*

CRITICISM ELICITS CHILDISH FEELINGS AND NEGATIVE THOUGHTS

Children often behave in ways that are unacceptable or even dangerous to themselves and others. Parents need to teach children not to break things, run into traffic, or hit the family dog. Criticism is one of the many tools parents use to control children, one that is frequently accompanied by threats and punishment. Parents may isolate children physically by sending them to their rooms, or emotionally through cold, aloof behavior.

As powerless children, we feel duly chastised by such treatment and in time learn to avoid many of the behaviors that elicit these responses in our parents. We don't always improve our behavior, but even when we do, feelings like guilt, anger, hurt, and anxiety do not disappear. So we carry over into adulthood the message that criticism means we have been bad, that we are inadequate. Rarely have we internalized the message that criticism can be anything other than a string of words that hurt.

Learning to understand our childish responses is the first step in turning criticism from a painful experience to be avoided at all costs into a valuable tool for improvement and growth.

Let's go back for a moment and examine Laura Brady's response to Dr. Meade. Laura was caught off guard by the doctor's surprise attack, so it's no wonder she felt threatened, no wonder her heart rate speeded up, her face flushed, her palms turned sweaty. She responded first by denying—she hadn't made the call, Ms. Murray did. Then she defended herself by trying to put the responsibility back on the doctor—last week he instructed her to call.

Neither tactic stopped Dr. Meade's attack on her. Faced with her failure to respond adequately and appease the doctor, Laura felt wounded and angry, unpleasant feelings for anyone. To save herself further discomfort, she decided to avoid dealing with Dr. Meade in the future. Steering clear of the volatile doctor may make Laura feel better, but it doesn't solve her problem. She will continue to be uncertain about the procedure he wants her staff to follow.

Her withdrawal gets Laura off the hot seat—for now. But in the long run no one wins, not Laura, not her nurses, not the doctor. It is easy to see, however, why Laura chose to avoid Dr. Meade. What self-respecting adult would volunteer for that kind of treatment?

Laura probably has never thought about her habitual responses to criticism, never examined the thought processes that led her to her decision. In similar circumstances, you probably haven't, either.

In my workshops the first exercise participants do is to look at their responses to criticism by answering five questions. This is your first exercise as well. But first I'd like you to know some of the typical responses to these questions.

WHO CRITICIZES YOU?

Criticism from almost anyone can cause discomfort: your boss, co-workers, your family, friends, the mechanic who fixes your car. Just about the only person I haven't heard mentioned is the milkman, and that's probably because few of us have milk delivered to our door these days.

Some people report that they can handle criticism

from one source but not another. A very successful attorney once told me that he can take criticism in a crowded courtroom without blinking an eye. But when his mother criticizes him, he immediately begins to stammer and feel guilty.

At work, people have difficulty when subordinates or less experienced workers criticize their job performance. Executives complain of being victimized by their colleagues' sarcasm. Others, afraid of losing their jobs or needing to do everything perfectly, are particularly alarmed by negative feedback from their boss.

At home, some who experience little discomfort when criticized on the job are unduly upset by criticism from a spouse, child, or brother or sister.

Obviously, we all have our own special reasons for the way we respond to certain critics, but knowing who our critics are enables us to formulate a strategy to deal with them.

WHAT ARE YOU CRITICIZED ABOUT?

Our critics take issue with the color of our shoelaces, our moral values, and everything in between. Just about anything we say or do can be a target of criticism from one person or another. And it's not unusual to get opposing views from different critics.

Take Joan, for instance, a bright, successful executive. Despite Joan's excellent performance, her boss constantly criticizes her for spending too little time on the job. When Joan goes home, however, her husband complains that she spends too much time at the office. Joan is ready to tear her hair out, and can you blame her?

Being aware of the specific things you are criticized for is important. Once you know the "whats," you can then go on to figuring out the "whys."

WHAT IS YOUR CRITIC'S INTENT?

Understanding your critic's motive is the key to choosing an appropriate response. There are just about as many reasons for criticizing as there are things to criticize; however, the reasons can be grouped into several distinct categories. As you can see from the following list, a critic's intent can be positive or negative. Critics can intend to:

Dominate and control
Manipulate
Put you down
Show compassion
Protect self-interest
Get a laugh at your
    expense
Abuse
Undermine
Get attention
Project their own faults
    onto you
Change you (even if
    you don't want to
    change)

Motivate growth
Improve a relationship
Punish/Get even
Distract you
Vent feelings
Show you who's boss
Communicate feelings
Show concern
Slice
Improve Performance

It may seem easy to examine your critic's words and fit them into one of these categories. Sometimes intent is apparent, but more often it is difficult to determine just what it is your critic really means to do. The difficulty is compounded by the fact that the critics themselves are often unaware of their intent.

For example, Lou walks in from work one evening and immediately lights into Alice, his wife, for being dressed in sloppy jeans and a tee-shirt. Alice, who has worked all morning at her part-time job and spent the afternoon looking after an infant and a toddler, yells back. When Lou cools off, he apologizes. He isn't really angry at Alice. Some unknown idiot plowed into his car in the plant parking lot and bashed in the fender.

Until Lou said something about the car, Alice might have thought he was being critical in order to put her down or undermine her, but his real intent was to vent his frustration about the car. Unfortunately for Alice— and for many on the receiving end of criticism—she bore the brunt of Lou's anger, even though she had been only its catalyst, not its cause.

We will examine intent more closely in Chapter 2. For now, it is enough to remember that intent is like an iceberg: there is often more below the surface than above. Learning how to decipher intent is one of the most important skills you will learn.

WHAT IS YOUR RESPONSE TO CRITICISM?

Most people respond to criticism with the childish behavior I call the Four Don'ts. They:

Defend
Deny
Counterattack
Withdraw

Why do we persistently respond to criticism in this way? We learned the Four Don'ts when we were first criticized when we were very young. With years of practice, we have gotten very good at these responses, which have become habit. Unfortunately, they are bad habits.

Nevertheless, we continue to use them. These responses worked (at least some of the time) when we were children, so we ignore the fact that they do not solve our adult problems. We also wish to alleviate immediately the discomfort that criticism brings. Never having learned any other ways of responding to criticism, we fall back on the ones at hand. In any critical situation we may use one or any combination or the Four Don'ts.

Recognizing the Four Don'ts will pave the way for replacing bad habits with good.

WHAT ARE YOUR FEELINGS?

I have rarely heard anyone say they felt good when criticized. They respond with the childish Four Don'ts and then feel belittled, guilty, angry, powerless, out of control, embarrassed, hurt, humiliated, ignorant, stupid, insignificant, etc., etc.

With feelings like those, no wonder we hate being criticized. If, however, we learn to change our thoughts and behavior when we are criticized, our negative feelings will change as well.

Let's take the case of Marian, the head of a high school art department. John, a teacher in her department, was unrelenting in his criticism of her. In turn, Marian defended herself or counterattacked. Her childish response empowered John and encouraged frequent attacks. She felt constantly victimized and eventually became very dissatisfied with her job, which she had previously enjoyed. As you can see, Marian's negative feelings about John's criticism had a far-reaching negative consequence.

Then Marian learned the technique of defusing, a way of cutting short a criticism and taking the sting out of it. Here are some of the responses Marian made to defuse John's criticisms:

John: "That skirt and blouse are frumpy; they're not fit for the head of an art department."
Marian: "I can see why you would say that."

John: "You mean to tell me you're scheduling another meeting? You sure are meeting-happy."
Marian: "It looks that way, doesn't it?"

John: "The pottery exhibit in your room looks as if it
was put on by preschoolers."

Marian: "Thank you for stopping by to take a look."

When Marian learned to defuse John's criticisms she
put herself in the adult position, where she was in control of herself. As a consequence of her new behavior,
her negative feelings diminished. John's attacks became
much less frequent, too. By empowering herself, Marian
had taken away the "fun" John got from criticizing her.

✔ *EXERCISE*

Now it's time for you to answer for yourself the five
questions we've just looked at. You will probably find
that you deal with many different critics who have different intents, to which you respond in different ways
and with different feelings.

Settle yourself comfortably in a quiet place where you
will not be disturbed. Take as much time as you need to
think carefully about and write out your responses to the
questions.

WHO	WHAT	CRITIC'S INTENT	MY RESPONSE	MY FEELINGS
Dr. M.	supervising my staff	vent his own anger	deny defend myself avoid him	humiliated furious powerless
Luke	not listening to him	help relationship	defend	self-righteous
Luke	being disorganized	put me down	counterattack	angry
Mom	house not tidy	show me she's still boss	attack her for butting in	guilty

WHO criticizes you?
WHAT do they criticize you about?
What is your critic's INTENT?
What is your RESPONSE?
What are your FEELINGS?

Writing down your answers in column form will give you an easy-to-see picture of your current responses to and feelings about criticism. Here is a sample table that Laura might have written to examine the episode with Dr. Meade (and exchanges with her husband, Luke, and her mother).

When you've completed your table, keep it handy; you will be referring to it in future exercises.

THE FOUR DON'TS

When held over into adulthood, childish behavior can have serious consequences. Let's look at each of the Four Don'ts and see how we undermine ourselves by continuing to rely on these responses.

✓ *DEFEND*

Children defend themselves against criticism to show powerful grown-ups that they are good and innocent of any wrongdoing. For children, not getting caught may mean they haven't done anything wrong. If, however, they do get caught, they try to prove that they have a good reason for their behavior. How else are they going to get their parents off their backs?

Here's how Joe defends himself to his father:

"Joe, I told you to vacuum and wash the car three days ago, and you still haven't done it. You don't follow through on your assignments. I always have to remind you."

"Dad, I've had band practice after school every

day this week. Then when I come home from school, I've got to set the table for dinner, eat dinner, put the garbage out and do my homework. I haven't had time to wash the car."

"You always have an excuse, son. You always have something else to do other than the jobs I give you."

"But, Dad, I have all those other things to do. I haven't had time for the car yet."

"You agreed to do the job, Joe."

"I know I agreed, but I didn't remember I had so many other things to do. And you didn't say you wanted it done so quickly."

Knowing he hadn't put a time limit on the job, Dad backs down. "All right. Just see to it that you wash the car in the next two days."

"Sure, Dad. I'll take care of it." As soon as Dad is gone, Joe lets out a loud sigh of relief. His fast talk worked. He got off the hook one more time.

Now, the question is, will Joe wash the car or will he come up with another set of excuses? If he doesn't wash the car his allowance may be docked or his television privileges curtailed, but he will still have a roof over his head and food on his plate.

But let's move ahead several years and substitute a report on the Blanchard project for washing the car, and Joe's boss for Joe's dad. Joe's fast-talking skills may help him out the first few times he misses a deadline, but unlike Joe's dad, his boss has no obligation to keep a roof over Joe's head or food on his plate. Joe's livelihood could soon be in jeopardy.

For adults, making excuses is simply not effective. In the professional world people don't want to know why the job hasn't been done, they just want it done. The more excuses we offer, the more foolish and childish we feel and appear.

Continual defense can lead our critics to suspect that we truly are guilty of something. And it can lead us to feel guilty even when we haven't made a mistake. No one likes feeling guilty, nor is it of any use to anyone. Instead of solving problems with our excuses, we compound them.

Defense also gets in the way of listening. To make criticism work for us, rather than against us, we first have to hear it. And we can't listen thoughtfully if we're busy making up excuses for ourselves.

✓   DENY

Denial is a great way for kids to slither out of a tight spot. Saying you didn't do whatever it is you did is almost as good as not having done it. It works often enough to make it a favorite ploy for children.

Timmy has climbed the kitchen stool and is standing on tiptoe with both hands in the cookie jar when he hears his mother approaching. Clutching his booty, he yanks his hands out of the jar and jumps off the stool.

"What are you up to, Timmy?" his mother calls. "Have you been at the cookies again? We already talked about that once today."

When Timmy hears that tone of voice he has no choice but to dive for cover. By the time she enters the room he is backing out the other door, his stash behind his back. "No way, Mom. I was just going to my room to do my homework." He makes a beeline for his room where he gobbles down all the cookies. Close call, he thinks, but I escaped. He's avoided being caught and punished, and that's all that counts.

But let's look at Tim as an adult. On his way home from work one night he stops to have a drink with a few friends. He walks in the front door forty-five minutes later than usual.

"You're late, Tim," his wife, Marcy, calls out from the kitchen. "I was getting worried. Where've you been?"

"I stayed late at work, that's all," Tim replies. Then he rushes upstairs and gargles with mouthwash. Down in the kitchen Marcy says nothing more about his coming in late. Still, he keeps his distance from her, all the while feeling more and more childish and foolish. Why am I acting this way? he asks himself. I should have told her I stopped for a drink with Charlie and Al. It's no big deal. I wasn't doing anything wrong.

But Tim feels as though he was caught with his hand in the cookie jar, so he responds with denial. Unfortunately, that puts Tim right back in the childish position he was in with his mother. But now he is an adult, and instead of feeling relieved, he feels like a fool.

The mouthwash story is true. A workshop participant took me aside during a break and sheepishly admitted it. Though the incident had occurred many months before, the blush on his cheeks told me he was still embarrassed and bothered by it.

Many times we issue a denial without thinking. Elaine did that and got herself into a demeaning situation.

"I haven't seen you working on the books this week," Elaine's boss says to her. "They have to be ready by the end of the month."

"I've been working on them," she responds, not admitting that she hasn't started the task. She prefers to do the books when she can set aside a large enough block of time to complete the work in one sitting, so she hasn't begun. But now, she has to keep the books open on her desk, and to remember to advance the pages, as if she is working on them, in order not to be caught in a lie.

If only Elaine had not explained her method of working, she wouldn't have to sneak around behind her boss' back.

Adults often make denials when all the other person wants is an honest answer to a question or to get a job done. By making an instinctive but childish response to a question or a reminder, we make ourselves look and feel ridiculous.

✓ *COUNTERATTACK*

Children unleash their uncensored thoughts and feelings because they have not yet learned rational thinking or mature problem-solving techniques. They strike back at their critics to win an argument; vent anger, anxiety, or frustration; or divert the critic's attention.

Frequently, children are successful in their counterattacks. They silence their critics and feel good in the bargain because they've vented their emotions.

As adults, we fall back on counterattack quite easily. Criticism heightens our emotions and stops rational thinking. All our hard-won communication skills fly out the window when we fly off the handle.

Matt is skilled at counterattack, especially with his younger brother Sam. Let's see how he uses the technique to win an argument about this year's family vacation.

"Let's go camping and mountain climbing this year," Matt proposes.

Sam puts in his bid. "I want to go to Disney World this year."

"That's stupid. Disney World is for sissies."

"That's not true, Matt. Besides, we went camping and hiking last year," Sam points out.

"Well, I want to go camping, and I'm the oldest."

"Just because you're the oldest you think you can have your own way all the time. That's not fair."

"So what?" Matt challenges. "You don't want to go climbing because you're clumsy and you're afraid you'll fall off a cliff. You're just a crybaby and a sissy. Only a sissy would want to go to Disney World."

"I am not a sissy!"

"Then prove it by going camping."

Sam doesn't have an answer to that one, so he backs off. Matt has learned that calling his brother names helps him get what he wants. He is thrilled. Sam will give up on his campaign to go to Disney World and the family will go camping again this year.

As an adult, Matt doesn't give up on the counterattack technique he learned as a child. He pulls the same routine with his wife, Christine, when she asks him to help her with the household chores.

"Housework is woman's work," Matt answers.

"I put in twelve hours a day between my job and taking care of the house. It's not fair for you to come home and put your feet up," Christine argues.

"I bring home more money. When you earn more than I do, I'll do the housework. How's that?"

"I'm not asking you to do all the chores, just to lighten the load for me."

Matt is tired of this discussion and decides to counterattack. "Look, I don't know why you keep making such a big deal about a little dusting and vacuuming. Why can't you complain about something important for once? You're nothing but a henpecker."

"And you're impossible!" Christine retorts and stomps out of the room.

Matt is pleased with himself. He got his wife off his back—this time. Eventually Christine may decide she can't stand living with a bully any longer and leave. Matt may have won the argument, but he could lose his marriage. He may not be aware that he is a bully, but he continues to behave like one because it gets him what he wants.

Counterattacking to win an argument may get us our way initially, but it blocks communication, builds resentment and often leads to hidden aggression by the victimized person, who may either withdraw or want to get even.

Children frequently counterattack as an outlet for strong emotions.

Richard is trying to learn to ride a bike. Time after time he falls off his new two-wheeler, bruising his knees as well as his pride. His older sister Kate rides up on her bike and offers to help.

It's bad enough that Richard can't ride his bike on his own, but seeing his sister doing what he can't makes him boil over. "Just leave me alone," he screams, "and mind your own business, you busybody!"

Kate shrugs her shoulders and rides off. Richard feels a little better because he's let off some steam. But he's no better off—he still can't ride his bike and now he has no one to help him learn.

Richard grows up and becomes an entrepreneur. He runs a chain of four retail stores in four different cities and is in the process of adding a fifth store in yet another city. Frustration is Richard's middle name. Employees don't show up. Merchandise doesn't arrive on time. Customers complain. The roof leaks. With each new "disaster" Richard screams and yells.

Richard has been fighting fires all day, driving from one city to another. It's the middle of August, the air-conditioning in his car has conked out. At closing time, he finally arrives at a branch store where he was supposed to be at noon. He's worried about a serious accounting problem and the assistant manager stops him to talk to him about the window displays.

"Why don't we hire a professional window dresser to display our merchandise?" the assistant manager proposes. "I don't think we're doing it very artistically ourselves."

"I didn't hire you to do things 'artistically,'" Richard says in a voice dripping with sarcasm. "Just leave the windows the way they are and concentrate on doing what I pay you for."

Richard has had a bad day; he's overwrought now, and distracted. But if he doesn't address the assistant manager's concern at another time, when he is calmer and can think, he has only added a management problem to the rest of his troubles.

Employees who work for bosses like Richard often report that they do their jobs without dedication or enthusiasm. They resent being screamed at, having their questions ignored and their ideas and suggestions disregarded. "Why can't he take a minute to listen to me?" they complain.

Counterattacking to vent anger or frustration may make us feel good for a moment or two, but it leaves us stuck with the same problem we started out with—or a bigger one.

Kids frequently counterattack to get adults off the track. It's a manipulative move, but it gets the ball out of their court just the same. For example:

Mom says to Jill, "It's your job to unload the dishwasher after school. You haven't done it once this week."

"You're not fair, Mom. I work hard all day in school and when I get home I deserve a chance to play. Donna's mother doesn't make her do her chores right after school."

Mom feels guilty and gives in. "All right, you can do it before dinner." But before dinner Jill has homework to do, and Mom ends up unloading the dishwasher herself.

Jill grows up and gets a job with a Fortune 500 company. But her work is not up to the standards of the firm. Her boss counsels her a number of times about improving her job performance. Jill has become very good at diverting a critic's attention, and manages to keep her job without substantially improving her work. For a while. The day finally comes when the boss realizes Jill is never going to perform up to standard and fires her.

Most people will agree that even though counterattack feels good initially, as a response to criticism it only causes awkwardness, embarrassment, and remorse. There are, however, those who extol the merits of a good straightforward attack. Why beat around the bush? they ask. Just tell it like it is.

But it is possible to be direct and to the point without mounting an attack. The techniques you will learn are all straightforward and honest, but they do not suggest attacking your critic.

In the examples of counterattack we've considered, the attackers chose to earn short-term points rather than strive for long-term wins. Matt got his wife off his back, but he may have jeopardized his marriage. Richard vented his frustrations, but he certainly lost the loyalty of his employee and probably lost business by not paying attention to his window displays. Jill got out of a ten-minute chore by diverting her mother's attention, but the same technique later lost her a lucrative and prestigious job.

Counterattack alienates, isolates, creates fear, blocks creativity and innovation. It also makes people want to get even. They do this by collecting what I call brown stamps.

Unlike green stamps, brown stamps are not redeemed for lampshades or waffle irons. They are hoarded as ammunition. Every time a person we work or live with shouts, intimidates us, puts us down, ignores us, tells us to do something because "I said so," and we comply, we have earned ourselves a brown stamp. When our pockets are brimming we cash them in, either passively or aggressively.

A passive redemption can be "forgetting" to pick up a spouse's re-strung tennis racket before the club tournament or making a colleague look bad by "losing" the only copy of an important report. An aggressive redemption can come in the form of an irate, seemingly unprovoked tirade, quitting a job without notice, or serving a spouse with divorce papers.

Let me tell you about some of my own brown stamps. About fifteen years ago, before I'd begun my work on criticism, I made an aggressive redemption of a whole fistful of brown stamps.

My then husband and I were seated in a marriage counselor's office, making a last stab at working out our differences. In the midst of an argument I thought of an incident that had nothing to do with the issue at hand. "You've been insensitive for years," I exclaimed and launched into a long, heated lecture. Since we married he had been comparing me—unfavorably—to local wives. Although I was raised in Staten Island, he wanted me not only to follow but to excel in the local customs of upstate New York.

"I'll never forget the time, about two years ago, when you came home with ten quarts of blackberries you'd bought at a roadside stand. You marched into the kitchen, plonked the boxes down on the counter and told me that a good Adirondack wife freezes at least ten blackberry pies every summer.

"At that point, I was trying to feed our eight-month-old, our toddler was underfoot, our three-year-old was tugging on me, demanding to be read a story, and you wanted me to bake ten blackberry pies! When I objected you looked at me and said, 'You mean you can't keep pace with other Adirondack women?' Then you started reading the newspaper. And now you wonder why I want a divorce!"

My husband looked puzzled. "Why didn't you tell me you were mad at the time and refuse to bake the pies?"

"I did tell you, but you didn't listen. You just hid behind your newspaper."

I should have persisted then, but I didn't. I baked the pies and stashed the brown stamps in my pocket. By the time I pulled them out, a few moths flew out with them.

So, the next time you are tempted to counterattack, consider the brown stamps you will create. The other person is sure to redeem them when you least expect it.

✓ *WITHDRAW*

The last of the Four Don'ts is also the last resort for many children when defense, denial, or counterattack doesn't work. They withdraw and remain silent when they feel helpless; when it's easier to accommodate than continue to press for what they want; when they can't get a word in edgewise; when they've learned that passive behavior brings peace or rewards, even if it does damage their sense of personal power and self-esteem.

When children—or adults—withdraw and remain silent they may also comply; seethe; plot; justify; or engage in negative interior monologues.

Children comply because it is the easy way out, because they fear rejection or punishment, or because they feel guilty.

Ken was raised by an extremely giving yet manipulative mother. She lavished a great deal of affection on her son and demanded his undying devotion in return. When the boy wanted to choose his friends and preferred other activities to spending time with her, she skillfully made him feel guilty. Afraid of losing his mother's love, Ken learned to withdraw and comply.

Today, Ken is a middle-aged bachelor. He has been dating a woman for years and wants to marry her, but he cannot because he cannot leave his mother. His mother has convinced him that she will die if he moves out of her house. Although Ken would like to have a life of his own, he has resigned himself to living with his mother. His woman friend is not satisfied with the arrangement and, though she cares for Ken, wonders how much longer she will stay in the relationship.

Silent compliance may bring a measure of peace to a child, but an unassertive adult like Ken loses his self-esteem and the ability to control the direction of his life. He may also appear indecisive, timid, fearful, or just plain boring.

Confronted with a battle they know they can't win, children often hold anger, frustration, or hurt in check. They slink away and seethe instead. The longer they hold in these powerful emotions, the less powerful children feel, despite using their withdrawal to punish the parent. Soon they are not only angry, frustrated, or hurt, they are wallowing in self-pity as well.

Take Debbie, for instance, a popular fifteen-year-old. She has been grounded for coming in late two weekends in a row. Her parents have called her rebellious, inconsiderate, and irresponsible, and she is deeply wounded. She sulks and sulks and sulks. That will show Mom and Dad. Besides, there is some small comfort in self-pity.

Ten years later, Debbie marries. She and her husband, Jack, have an argument. Debbie is not good at arguing and she lets Jack do most of the talking. In his anger he calls her ungrateful, uncaring, inconsiderate, and passive. Debbie feels hurt by his attack, but does not express her true feelings. She withdraws and seethes. She withholds warmth and affection, which upsets Jack. The relationship suffers. Debbie suffers, too. Her unexpressed anger builds up and sends her into a depression. Soon the barriers to honesty and intimacy are so great that the relationship fails.

We are the ones who suffer most when we withdraw and seethe. Restrained, unexpressed anger frequently takes a toll on our mental and physical well-being. Learning to deal with others in a direct, straightforward way may not always be easy, but it is a good deal easier than living with the effects of silent seething.

One way children restore their sense of personal power after a confrontation is to plot ways to get even. Some find their fantasies satisfying enough, while others carry out their plans.

Frank's father tells him to clean the garage, now.

"But, Dad, there's a football game at school in an hour. Can't I do it later?"

"I said now."

"But, Dad—"

"Now!" The edge in Dad's voice could split a log.

Frank cleans the garage. He's going to miss the game anyway, so he takes four hours to do a two-hour job. Part of the reason it takes him so long is that he moves all of his father's tools around, so that Dad won't be able to find a thing. And he's done the job so badly that Dad will have to go over it himself.

Frank becomes an engineer and goes to work for a manufacturing firm. His boss there doesn't like to be questioned any more than Frank's father liked it. The boss gives Frank an assignment. "I don't think that's the best way to go about it," Frank objects.

"Do it and do it now," the boss says.

"But I really think we'd get better results—"

"I told you to do it. I know what I'm talking about. I don't have time to convince you."

Frank completes the assignment, but his work is half-hearted. He takes too much time to do the job and it is far from perfect when completed. There isn't much else Frank can do to get his revenge, but even these small gestures don't make him feel good. He knows his work could be much better, but he just can't motivate himself to do good work for such a jerk of a boss. Not only is Frank unhappy, but the company is left with a shoddy product to sell. Frank's self-esteem suffers, the company suffers, and Frank's future is at stake.

Clearly, nobody wins.

Children justify their actions to themselves in order to avoid feeling that they are bad or wrong. The positions they take may well be legitimate, but children don't express themselves openly for fear that the powerful adult will prove them wrong or punish them. So, they justify in silence.

Sylvia does not want to go to summer camp. When she protests, her parents criticize her for being a baby. Chastened, she does not tell her parents she is afraid of being away from home for such a long time. Full of fear, she goes off to camp, which she hates. Not only is she far from home, but there are bugs and crawly things; the other girls in her cabin were campers together the previous summer and she feels left out.

She asks her parents to let her come home, but they tell her she has to give camp another chance. But she doesn't want to do that, so out of sheer misery she either deliberately or unconsciously misbehaves, to the point where she is so disruptive the camp must send her home.

Sylvia's parents are now as angry and disappointed with her as she was with them for sending her away. But she still doesn't express her feelings openly. She withdraws from their criticism, silently justifying her behavior. Who could have expected her to behave well when camp was full of creepy, crawly frightening things and girls who made fun of her?

Years later, Sylvia and her brother Mike buy a bookstore from its retiring owner. Mike wants to keep the shop very much as it is, a leisurely, old-fashioned place that caters to browsers and book-lovers. Sylvia is convinced they will never be able to compete with the new store a national chain is opening in a nearby shopping center if they don't give over some of their floor space to magazines and gift items. On her own she orders the items she wants.

Mike is livid and sends the order back. He criticizes Sylvia for not consulting him and tries to get Sylvia to explain to him why she went behind his back. She withdraws, silently justifying herself as having done the best thing for the business. Sylvia and Mike never solve their differences about what's best for the store. Whether from competition from the new chain store or competition between the partners, the venture fails.

Who knows? The bookstore might have been a success if Sylvia had had the courage of her convictions and convinced Mike to try out a line of magazines and gift items. But once she went behind his back, she had very little chance of seeing her plan succeed.

Very often, our opinions and ideas have a great deal of merit. But if we keep them—and our feelings—to ourselves, we not only prevent our personal growth but also hinder our effectiveness in our workplace or the success of our relationships.

When children make mistakes and are criticized, they often internalize the observations of their critics. They say to themselves, "Mom's right, I sure am clumsy," or, "I *am* stupid at math, just like Mr. Allport says. I'll never get these problems right." A harshly self-critical interior monologue does nothing for a child's sense of worth or accomplishment. Or an adult's, for that matter.

Take ten-year-old Russell, a precocious child with a gift for words. One summer he decides to start a neighborhood newspaper. He scours the block to gather news, painstakingly types his stories, makes copies, and distributes the paper. When his father, a demanding perfectionist, comes home, Russell proudly presents him with a copy of his newspaper. Father reads it, points out his spelling and grammatical errors, and without a single word of praise goes off to fix himself a perfect dry martini. Russell takes his hurt out on himself, telling himself how dumb he is for misspelling Mr. Clarke's name.

Russell grows up to become a talented political speechwriter. He is well known and his services are in constant demand. But when his speeches are criticized he breaks out in a cold sweat. He then engages in negative self-talk, asking himself things like, "Why can't I do it exactly the way the Senator wants it the first time around?" and, "How could I have mixed up the figures on those trade statistics?" Instead of using his considerable intelligence and energy to correct his mistakes and move on, Russell wastes valuable time beating himself up.

There is certainly merit in the desire to excel and to work hard to accomplish our goals. But when exaggerated, this desire can be debilitating. Imperfection is the one trait we share with every other human being in the world. Excessive, constant negative self-talk is nothing less than an attempt to drum ourselves out of the human corps. The next time you try to talk yourself into being perfect, think about what a freak you would be if you succeeded.

We have seen throughout this chapter that criticism is hard to take mainly because we respond to it like children. Criticism represents danger, so we think of it as a threat and respond by falling back on the Four Don'ts. We defend ourselves, deny responsibility, counterattack or withdraw. These childish responses are accompanied by childish feelings of powerlessness, guilt, anger, frustration, fear, anxiety, none of which helps us to handle ourselves effectively.

Not only do we feel out of control when we respond to criticism this way, we inadvertently empower our critics. Compound all this with a negative thought process and the picture gets gloomier and gloomier.

One way to brighten this picture is to replace our old habitual responses with new ones that enable us to maintain our adult control. Changing the way we think about criticism helps us to change our feelings and responses and reinforces our new good habits.

Instead of criticizing ourselves or attacking our critics, we can learn to think over criticism objectively, then choose an appropriate response. Instead of letting criticism make victims of us, we can use it to empower ourselves. Instead of fighting feelings of powerlessness and frustration, we can embrace criticism as a powerful ally for growth, change, and fulfillment.

2

Intent:
Understanding Your Critic's
Motives

YOU CANNOT COPE effectively with criticism if you do
not understand your critic's intent. Knowing why your
critic is criticizing you helps you choose the appropriate
response.

Different people criticize you at different times for
different reasons. In the morning your sister may criticize you to spare you the anguish of making a mistake in
a major life decision. That afternoon that same sister
may pass a cutting remark out of jealousy. Understanding her motivation will either tell you to listen carefully
to what she has to say and use that information as you
make your choice or tell you to disregard her comment,
recognizing that even though she loves you, she has
fallen back into old patterns of vying for parental love
and attention.

THE ICEBERG OF INTENT

Intent is best likened to an iceberg: the jagged peak
jutting out of the water gives only a small hint of what
lies underneath.

Just as the tip of an iceberg is visible to the naked eye,

so critical behavior can easily be seen and observed. To examine an iceberg's hidden structure, however, scientists need sophisticated instruments. In the same way, we need sophisticated techniques to inspect and determine the often elusive motivation behind critical behavior.

Understanding intent can be as difficult for your critic as for you. Motivation is often so elusive that a critic may not be consciously aware of what he or she is doing. The true intent may be so repressed that your critic may not see it or believe it even when it is pointed out.

To help you learn to decipher intent, I have chosen to use as examples a number of the most common reasons why people criticize. I will define each of these intents and introduce a case history drawn from my work experience that illustrates it. As we move on to learning the techniques, we'll follow these same people to show how they implemented the techniques. (The names of these people have been changed to preserve their anonymity.) We'll start with negative intent first, then move on to positive.

NEGATIVE INTENT

✓ *DOMINATE / CONTROL*

People who use criticism to dominate want to put themselves in a commanding position. They want to stand above you and enhance their own power by putting you on the defensive. How many times have you seen a meeting or a conversation disrupted by someone who interrupts, challenges, and criticizes your presentation or ideas before you've had a chance to state your entire case? If you stop what you are doing to make excuses or answer your critic, you are allowing that critic to assume a powerful, dominant position.

Not everyone who is dominant is controlling, how-

ever. Many people have the stature, charisma, and forcefulness that make them natural leaders, but their
dominance is based on the way they present themselves
and the work they do, not on their ability to keep others
down. In fact, many people are dominant because they
have the gift of bringing out the best in others.

But beware of people who use their strength and
forcefulness to intimidate you and foist their ideas on
you. Their critical behavior is meant to enhance their
position, not to help you.

Those who use criticism to control want to regulate,
check, or restrain another person. Parents necessarily do
this frequently to children. When adults do it to each
other, their motives bear investigation. Pat Lamb, a
well-respected marriage counselor, said to me in a recent
interview: "Controlling people often use criticism to
keep the world running their way." They don't criticize
to help others or improve relationships, but to ensure
that things are done the "right way," that is, their way.

There are some controllers I call bulldozers. They are
hostile, aggressive, intimidating, loud, overwhelming,
unrelenting, and rude. Bulldozers need to prove to themselves and the world that they are right. They appear
extremely confident because they frequently get their
way. To a bulldozer, the appearance of success is very
important. And on the surface, things usually look fine.
If bulldozers looked deeper, however, (which they generally do not) they would find that they lack friends and
real respect. Because they refuse to listen, other people
find it difficult—almost impossible—to be honest with
bulldozers. Their long-term relationships sometimes
erode.

These abrasive, difficult controllers lack the capacity
to listen to and accept criticism about their impact on
others. Their controlling behavior is the source of their
security and power. Examining that behavior might

mean giving it up, and bulldozers certainly do not want to do that. Robert M. Bramson states in his book *Coping with Difficult People* (Ballantine Books, New York, 1981), "They possess tremendous power in interpersonal situations. Such power comes largely from the typical responses their behavior arouses: confusion, mental or physical flight or a sense of helpless frustration that leads to tears or tantrum-like rage."

It is important to learn to stand up to this type of person, to keep yourself from being run over by a bulldozer. All the coping techniques you will learn are helpful with this type of critic.

Let's look at some other reasons why people use criticism to dominate and control. Sue, a successful professional woman, attempts to control by completely organizing household chores and activities, showing her co-workers how to do things, arranging social events to her own exacting standards. Sue's father was an alcoholic. Because she never knew what to expect as a child she tries to control everything in her life, including people.

Sue's husband, Guy, brought this behavior to her attention. She thought about his criticism and realized the source of her behavior. Now Sue is working to be less critical and controlling of her family and colleagues.

Some people seek to dominate and control because they have been told since childhood that their rightful position is on top. They think of themselves as more intelligent and clever than anyone else, so naturally they must see that their ideas prevail. They are extremely critical of anyone who does not do things their way. These people are often quite accomplished, but their critical behavior alienates fellow professionals, employees, and loved ones. This is clearly the case with Anna and George.

George is an extremely successful entrepreneur who

built a multimillion-dollar company from the ground floor. In any relationship, George believes himself to be the smartest and most capable. Because of his good looks, athletic ability, and popularity, he grew up having an unrealistic sense of entitlement and thinking he should get his way all the time. Because George is intelligent and forceful he has been able to dominate and control Anna throughout their twenty-one-year marriage. Nevertheless, she is devoted to him and their two sons. But she knows she must find a way of standing up to George's criticism.

I met Anna when she joined an assertivensss support group I was leading. Because of her long years of giving in to George, her self-esteem was low, but she was determined to improve. One way she felt she could bolster her self-image was to exercise and lose weight. So she devised an exercise program. She would do a combination of running and walking three mornings a week with some women from the group, and she would sign up for tennis instruction.

George criticized her choice, telling her she needed a stricter, more demanding program. Then he went ahead and enrolled her in an aerobics class that met every weekday at the local Y. Although Anna feels comfortable with her program, George continues to insist that she do what he wants. We will follow Anna's progress as she uses the various coping techniques to help her deflect George's criticism and do what is right for her.

✓ MANIPULATE

Manipulators use criticism to induce guilt in others. Very often manipulators use phrases like "you never" or "you always" or "so-and-so does this and you don't." Manipulators want to get their own way, but they don't use a simple, direct, adult mode of communication to get it.

A manipulative wife who feels her husband is not spending enough time with his family will not say, "I want you to spend more time with me and the kids." Instead she says things like, "You never spend any time with us." Or, "Dan took Ellen and the boys to the ball game on Saturday. You never do that for us." Neither communication assures that the wife will get her husband to spend more time with the family. The non-critical, direct statement, however, opens the door to communications. The manipulative, critical statement closes it.

Let's take a look at the case of Tom, a middle-aged doctor, and his mother, Jenny. Jenny believes Tom does not pay her enough attention. Instead of saying to her son, "I would like you to call and visit me more often," she criticizes him indirectly by comparing him, unfavorably of course, to the son of a friend of hers who is able to spend significantly more time with his mother. These comparisons imply that Tom is not thoughtful and does not demonstrate his love for her.

Tom does love his mother, but the circumstances of his life are different from those of Bruce, the son of his mother's friend. For one thing, Tom lives three hundred miles away from his mother; Bruce lives in the same city as his mother. Tom is married and has three children; Bruce and his wife have no children. But Jenny does not take into account these genuine differences that affect Tom's availability to her. The coping techniques Tom learns help him both to deal with his mother's constant criticism and to show his genuine concern for her.

✓   *PUNISH / GET EVEN*

When people feel injured or unfairly treated they often resort to criticism as a means of punishing or getting even. Because they have been hurt, they want the other person to hurt, too. Sometimes these critics retaliate in private, but often they choose a public forum to get their digs in, hoping to make their remarks more hurtful.

Even in loving relationships, partners may use criticism to punish or get even when they feel they are not being listened to or taken seriously. I observed a clear example of this in the case of Mary and Bill.

Like all happily married couples, Bill and Mary have their disagreements from time to time. A long-running disagreement for them is how many hours Bill puts in at work each week. Mary thinks he is spending far too much time at the office; Bill believes he must devote a great deal of time to his profession in order to build his career. Mary loves and cares for Bill deeply, and her feelings are reciprocated. But this does not stop Mary from making remarks like, "Bill doesn't know what the children look like anymore." When asked if they would like to attend a social event, Mary might say, "Well, we'll have to see if Bill can stop working long enough."

Clearly, this is Mary's way of punishing Bill for not being around more often. Bill, however, resents being punished for doing what he feels he must to ensure his family's financial security and to honor his commitment to high professional standards. By learning how to cope with Mary's punishing remarks, Bill puts their otherwise good relationship back on a firm footing. He maintains his equilibrium and thus avoids building anger and resentment.

✓ *ABUSE*

Punishment becomes abuse when it increases in intensity and frequency. For example, if a child misbehaves and is sent to his room to sit alone for half an hour, that is punishment. If he misbehaves and is isolated day after day for long periods of time, that is abuse.

Abuse occurs when one person controls or subjugates another through humiliation, fear, intimidation, and physical or verbal assaults. People don't have to use their fists to abuse one another. Words and mood swings are powerful weapons.

Any relationship in which the attacks are sharp, venomous and personal is abusive. A very interesting case is that of Margaret, a member of one of my support groups, and her husband, Bob. Bob never raised a hand against his wife, but he abused her nonetheless.

Margaret, a twenty-nine-year-old magazine editor, met Bob, a forty-six-year-old businessman, while he was in Manhattan on a business trip. Margaret found Bob attractive, charming, intelligent, and confident. He apparently was drawn by those same qualities in her. Although Margaret had some initial misgivings about the difference in their ages, after a year-long whirlwind courtship she married Bob, gave up her job, and moved to his home in upstate New York. As they both wanted to have a child right away, Margaret had decided not to look for work outside the home, but to start a new career as a free-lance writer and editor.

Only after their honeymoon did Margaret begin to see Bob's "other side." When Bob came home in the evening he did not take off his boss hat. He wanted to run things, the same way he did in his business. He tried to tell Margaret how to shop, cook, do the laundry, load the dishwasher. No matter what she did, he had a better way of doing it. Even cleaning the kitchen counter. When she snapped back at him, saying "I don't need to do it your way to get the counter clean," his comeback was twice as loud and twice as strong.

He frequently denigrated her abilities, whether to clean the kitchen counter, to succeed in her new profession, or, after their daughter was born, to be a mother.

He challenged her opinions about politics, philosophy, and religion, calling her stupid or ridiculous if she did not agree with his point of view or could not immediately substantiate her opinion with specific quotes from experts.

Although she had considered herself a confident, assertive woman before her marriage, living with Bob's constantly abusive criticism caused Margaret to doubt herself and her abilities. The other problem with Bob was his Jekyll-and-Hyde nature. He could be as charming and loving a husband and father one day as he had been nasty and abusive the day before. He frequently told Margaret she was responsible for his behavior, and because Bob was so forceful, she eventually began to wonder if he was right, if in fact she was the monster in their marriage.

Margaret was unrelenting in her attempts to decipher the intent behind Bob's criticism. Initially, she came up with the answer that he was used to being the boss at work and did not want to give up that control when he got home. But this answer did not totally satisfy her. Bob's actions were too extreme for just wanting to be the boss.

She tried to get to the next layer of the iceberg by talking to Bob's family and business associates. She discovered he was just as controlling and demanding with them. He expected everyone in the world to treat him with the doting deference his mother had given him. And for the most part, he behaved in ways that made people bend to his will.

But, Margaret asked next, why was Bob so sarcastic? Why did he put people down so frequently? Why did he challenge everyone, even in casual conversations? She finally realized that beneath Bob's bravado he was terribly insecure. His inner fears created his dominating, controlling, and at times abusive behavior.

As she put the pieces of the puzzle together, Margaret realized that she was not the monster Bob tried to get her to believe she was. The monster was buried deep inside Bob. Unfortunately, he could not be persuaded to take a careful look at himself, to uncover and examine the internal ghosts that held so much power over him.

Margaret believed there was enough in her marriage to make it worth salvaging, and because of their daughter she wanted very much to make the relationship work. Understanding the intent behind Bob's criticism helped Margaret to be a bit more patient with Bob and his mood swings, but to cope effectively with his behavior she had to regain the confidence she had lost and learn to reassert herself. The coping techniques were instrumental in helping Margaret work on her very difficult problem.

✓ PROJECT / TRANSFER

Sometimes critics criticize others for something they do themselves. They repudiate an unpleasant, unwanted characteristic by projecting it onto you. Most people who do this do it unconsciously. They are not aware that the undesirable trait is their own. Nor are they likely to recognize this behavior, even if you try to point out that they are accusing you of doing what they themselves actually do. It is, however, helpful for you to be aware of projection and how it works.

Bob, as well as being abusive in his criticism, frequently projected his characteristics onto Margaret. He often told Margaret she was spoiled and self-centered and did not think about him. But Margaret believed Bob was the one who was spoiled and self-centered and did not think about her.

When she talked to family and friends, their experiences with Bob confirmed her own belief: Bob was the

spoiled, self-centered partner in their relationship. But
he was unable to recognize or accept those traits in himself. Yet they were there, so he conveniently projected
them onto Margaret. The coping techniques helped Margaret deal with this aspect of Bob's critical behavior as
well as his abusiveness.

✓ *SLICE*

Slicers—you may also have heard them called
nibblers or put-down artists—chip away at other people
in an attempt to enhance their own stature. They mistak-
enly believe that cutting down other people makes them
look taller.

People in subordinate positions are not the only ones
who turn to slicing. Many managers, even heads of companies, do their share of cutting down in a misguided
attempt to keep others from threatening or horning in on
their position. Others slice because they learned it from
their parents, who used it to keep both their children and
each other down. These slicers never learned to relate to
people in any other way, and may slice more out of habit
than to belittle.

Slicers say things that tend to diminish you, leaving
you with less power, confidence, and self-esteem. This is
what happened to Cynthia, a computer scientist, when
she encountered Stan on the job at the Wall Street of-
fices of a well-known international bank. Stan and Cynthia were peers, but Stan had been at the bank for about
a year when Cynthia arrived.

Almost from day one, Stan made derogatory comments about Cynthia's work, clothes, and moods. He
said things like, "This isn't really your area of expertise,
is it?" Or, "Where did you dig up that outfit?" Or,
"You're too sensitive."

He also put down women in general with remarks

like, "We couldn't expect a woman to figure that out." And, "The best place for a woman in this bank is behind a teller's window."

Stan was a thorn in Cynthia's side and dampened her enthusiasm for her job until she participated in a workshop on criticism offered by her firm's human resources department. There, she learned to tip the scales in her working relationship with Stan.

✓ *GET ATTENTION*

Attention-seekers criticize to turn the spotlight on themselves. A critical comment will usually get some sort of answer, which automatically puts the critic in a superior position. They delight in any attention that can be turned their way and may not always be aware that criticism is the means by which they are getting the attention they crave.

Frequently attention-seekers nit-pick to get into the limelight. By choosing to attack on a minor issue, they divert attention from the business at hand and onto themselves.

Jonathan, a manager at a large corporation, had a problem with Herb, an attention-seeker. At meetings, Herb pounced on small details of a presentation before Jonathan had finished stating his case. Even during idle chitchat at lunch, Herb challenged Jonathan. If Jonathan talked about a magazine article he'd read, Herb had read one that was better or that contradicted Jonathan's article.

Jonathan was uncomfortable with Herb's constant challenges but didn't know how to stop the attention-seeking maneuvers. Once he learned the coping techniques, however, he was able to take an adult position and retain his proper place in the spotlight.

✓ *CHANGE YOU*

Changers pick a rose and wish they had a gardenia. They are not satisfied with who you are and want to change you, even if you don't need or want to change. They tell you to act differently, to think differently; they want you to conform to their image of you.

Tony, a financial planner for a large Midwestern company, married a changer. Soon after the wedding, his wife, Jane, took on the task of reshaping Tony. She started with his clothing. She told him his clothes were boring and conservative and that he should "get with it." She began to go shopping with him and picked out styles Tony never would have chosen himself.

Before his marriage, Tony had been quite comfortable with the way he dressed. His clothes suited his personality and were appropriate for both his professional and his leisure activities. But for part of the year the marriage lasted he tried to suit his tastes to Jane's, even though he felt uncomfortable in the new clothes, especially at the office, where they were quite conspicuous.

Jane was not content with changing Tony's appearance; she wanted to change his personality as well. When they attended social functions related to Tony's work, she criticized him for being too shy and retiring. He did not mingle enough, she said; he would never get ahead.

At first, as he had done with his clothes, Tony tried to please Jane. But soon after she went to work on his personality, he realized he had a serious problem. He decided to seek help from a therapist. Jane was vehemently opposed to his doing so, but he went anyway. He became stronger and less acquiescent, and Jane threatened to leave him if he didn't drop the sessions with his "meddling" therapist. Tony continued to see the therapist, and eventually the marriage broke up.

Jane is an extreme example of a changer. Most are not so blatantly obvious and try to work on only one or two aspects of you. Still, you should not let anyone force you into changing unless you are certain the change is right for you.

✔ *SHOW YOU WHO'S BOSS*

Some people use criticism to establish and maintain a superior position in the pecking order. They try to get you to defend yourself and answer to them, so that it is clear to everyone involved—bystanders as well as you and your critic—"who's the boss."

The I'm-the-boss syndrome is often encountered in first-time managers. These new managers are like a new kid on the block who promises himself not to let anyone push him around. To cover for their insecurities they become critical and demanding. Some experienced managers fall into the same trap, never having learned the skills that will enable them to direct their staff without having to rule the roost.

Kimberley, an account executive, had a manager, Alex, who seemed to go out of his way to criticize her for insignificant details. He did this even in areas where she clearly had more knowledge and expertise. When there was more than one way of accomplishing a task, he implied strongly that his method was superior. Alex's intrusive carping made Kimberley lose respect for him. She realized that she never really listened to him, even when his criticism might help her solve a problem. Learning to cope with Alex's "bossism" not only made Kimberly feel better about her job, it made her and Alex a better working team.

✔ *GET YOU OFF THE TRACK*

Politicians are a good example of this kind of critic: the counterattacker. If politician A questions politician B's view on a certain issue, B is more likely to respond with an attack on A than with a discussion of the issue. We see this in the press frequently.

At work, counterattackers get their managers off the track by saying things like, "Why are you singling me out when everybody in this department does the same thing?" Or, "I've seen you do that, too." The counterattacker may have a legitimate basis for what he says, but he does not say it to foster improvement. All he wants is to get out from under the pressure of being criticized.

Jim, a newly promoted manager, was concerned about Steve. Jim and Steve had gotten along fine when they were co-workers, but since Jim's promotion Steve had been difficult to deal with. Jim understood that Steve might be jealous of or resent his promotion, but Steve was letting this undermine his job performance.

When Jim called Steve into his office to discuss areas of Steve's work that needed improvement, Steve would counter Jim's suggestions with remarks like, "Oh, get off my back. You used to do the same thing." And, "I see you're giving your old buddies a hard time just because you're the manager now."

By defending himself or making excuses, Jim frequently got off the track. Jim found this very frustrating and began to avoid dealing with Steve. Work and morale in Jim's section were suffering. As the manager, he knew it was up to him to solve the problem.

✓ UNDERMINE

In his book *Coping With Difficult People*, Dr. Robert M. Bramson calls people who undermine "snipers." Sniping is a passive-aggressive way of criticizing. It is indirect, appearing as gossip, backbiting, or a cutting remark delivered in sweet, conciliatory tones. A sniper may appear concerned when saying, "Now, we all know that Paul is new at this job. So we can't expect too much, can we?" But the sniper's real intent is to gain power and leverage through the camouflaged criticism.

Rita, a woman who has achieved a great deal of success and recognition in the business community, was the victim of a sniper early in her career. Sally, another woman in her department, and Rita were both being considered for an advanced position that was about to open up. In face-to-face dealings, Sally always appeared to be very nice. But behind Rita's back, Sally challenged

Rita's decisions and capabilities in discussions with other staff members. Sally was so skilled at sniping that it took Rita many months to realize that Sally was out to get her. Rita remembers one particular incident only too well.

Rita had purchased a new suit and wore it to work for the first time. "Rita, honey, where did you buy that suit?" Sally asked when Rita came into the office that morning. Rita gave her the name of the store. "My goodness, darling," Sally cooed, "that is the cutest little thing. You look as though you could step right on a plane and take one of their hostess jobs."

Rita never wore the suit again.

Sally did not succeed in undermining Rita's career with her sniping, but she might have. Fortunately, there are ways to prevent snipers from aiming at you.

✓   *VENT FEELINGS*

Venters take out their feelings of anger or frustration on unsuspecting and undeserving recipients. We've all heard kids warn, "Watch out for Dad. He's in a bad mood." Sometimes a venter is only that—someone who's had a bad day and is letting off steam. Like Lou, who criticized his wife's appearance after finding his car had been damaged in the plant parking lot. Once in a while, we take out our frustrations on the unlucky person who happens to be standing next to us. Sometimes, when we cool down, we realize what we've done and apologize.

When you are on the receiving end of a vent, it's important not to take it personally. Try to take a step away from the situation and realize that the other person needs to blow off some steam to get her thoughts and feelings back into balance.

There are, however, some people whose primary way of venting their feelings is through criticism. They blow up and criticize most of the time and can only rarely express their feelings any other way. Fran, a line manager for a small but rapidly expanding manufacturing company, had a boss like that. Martin erupted frequently but unpredictably. His critical outbursts confused Fran and kept her off balance.

By taking time to look at Martin's intent closely, Fran realized that he was under a great deal of pressure from above. The firm's owners were hoping to make a public stock offering soon and were leaning heavily on Martin to keep up production levels. Martin, in turn, was taking it out on Fran. This might have helped Martin cope, but it put Fran in an uncomfortable position, making it difficult for her to keep her job and her sanity.

✓ GET ONE'S OWN WAY

Some people become harsh critics the second they suspect they are not going to get exactly what they want exactly when they want it. They seem to have no end of feelings to vent. I call these people "short fuses." They tend to be spoiled, intolerant people who believe they are entitled to have everything their way.

Sarah realized that she and her children were constantly tiptoeing around her husband, Larry. He didn't want the children to have their friends around because it disturbed him. His friends, of course, could come over whenever he wanted them to. He didn't allow the kids to play the music they liked, but he could play his music as loud as he wanted it. He demanded a quiet, orderly household and if he didn't get it, he criticized Sarah and the children unmercifully.

Sarah examined the intent behind Larry's criticism and decided that Larry's behavior was due to his being spoiled and having an exaggerated sense of entitlement. His outbursts were frequent, but he wasn't just venting anger or frustrations with them. He was really demanding his own way.

When Larry was growing up his mother had solved every problem, large or small, in her son's life. She had taught him that he was so wonderful and so special he did not have to put up with the same frustrations and discomforts as ordinary mortals. According to the world view Larry learned, he deserves his way no matter what, and the person who tries to thwart him must be punished and learn to toe the line.

Sarah had a long struggle to change Larry's pattern of behavior, but the coping techniques helped her and the children stand up for their right to enjoy their own home.

✓ *GET A LAUGH*

Critical comments can sometimes get a laugh, particularly when the joke is at someone else's expense. Dr. Joel Goodman, director of the Humor Project in Saratoga, New York, calls this "toxic humor." We see it in ethnic and sexist jokes, sarcasm, and put-downs.

The obvious intent of using toxic humor is to get a laugh. But if we examine the iceberg, we find many other motivations: to relieve tension, cope with problems, get attention, punish or feel superior by pointing out and laughing at the foibles and shortcomings of others. After all, we are all full of imperfections. They are easy enough to find and make fun of.

At its worst, toxic humor is used to release aggression and hostility. Dr. Goodman believes some people engage in toxic humor because it is a way of being one of the gang. "But who wants to engage in gang warfare?" he asks.

Most people who engage in toxic humor do not enjoy it as much as it would seem. They overwhelmingly admit that they are uncomfortable with sarcasm and jokes that succeed at someone else's expense, especially theirs. So why do they do it? Because it is the "thing to do," not because they enjoy it.

Looking at the light side of things is always welcome —even, perhaps especially, in serious situations. And witty, good-natured banter exchanged among equals is an important ingredient in successful personal and professional relationships. But humor that belittles or demeans any individual or group is far from useful. Jules Feiffer, noted cartoonist, playwright and 1986 Pulitzer Prize winner, offers an excellent insight on toxic humor: "Sarcasm and put-downs are so easy, such an easy way to get a laugh. I hear so many ridiculous questions from audiences—young people especially—a quick shot would be so easy. I resist it. It's cheap and in the long run no good. Put-downs and sarcasm keep people at arm's length."

In later chapters, we'll take a look at what you can do to stop toxic humor.

It is possible to draw a conclusion from the examples we've looked at: criticism motivated by a negative intent does not produce growth. Instead, the victims of negative intent often end up with diminished power, status, and self-esteem. We have seen in many of our case histories just how destructive these intents can be. Under the force of Bob's abusive criticism and his attempt to project his undesirable traits onto her, Margaret lost her self-confidence and the ability to assert herself. Jane and Tony's marriage crumbled under the weight of Jane's attempts to change Tony. Jim's effectiveness as a manager was undermined by Steve's maneuvers to get him off the track.

On the other hand, criticism spurred by a positive intent, expressing concern or a desire to solve a problem, can produce growth. It empowers and enhances both status and self-esteem. When criticism has a positive intent and delivery, both parties benefit in improved performance, better communication, more fulfilling personal relationships.

Let us now take a closer look at some of the positive motivations behind criticism.

POSITIVE INTENTS

What is the single most important indicator for determining whether intent is positive or negative? Delivery. Is the criticism given in a way that invites you to grow? Or does it slap you down and leave you feeling powerless or belittled?

Jan and Chuck, colleagues in a software development firm, are working on a project along with two other people. Chuck gets an idea and orders some expensive materials without telling his colleagues. When Jan realizes what he has done, she is irritated. In the past, Chuck has made and acted on decisions without consulting the rest of the team. Now he's done it again.

Frustrated at having what she thought was a past problem surface once more, Jan storms into his office. "Chuck, there you go again, making decisions as if you're the only person working on this project. You sure don't know how to work well with others!"

Now let's take the same situation once again. Jan feels the same irritation but pauses to think for a few moments before going to Chuck's office. Even though she'd love to vent her feelings, she recognizes that won't solve the problem. So she calms herself down, thinks, and then enters Chuck's office. "Chuck, the other day you ordered some expensive materials without consulting me or the rest of the team. I felt left out. I'm also puzzled about why you think we need those materials. I'd like all of us to be in on ordering extra materials. That way we'd be more productive and work better as a team."

In the first scenario, Jan's delivery is clearly aimed at venting her frustrations while cutting down Chuck at the same time. In the second, her delivery is aimed at solving a problem in communication and improving the working relationship.

It is very important to learn to recognize positive intent. We are so conditioned to react to any criticism with

the Four Don'ts that we can easily miss out on the benefits of criticism. Once we can tell when our critic is on
our side—the side of the relationship or of problem-
solving—we can open ourselves up to what is being said
and reap the full benefit of the critical comments.

✓ *IMPROVE PERFORMANCE*

Criticism is an integral part of the work world. No
matter what your job, you can be sure that if your performance is not up to snuff, you will hear about it.

The performance appraisals that are standard operating procedure at many organizations are a perfect example of regular feedback that can help employees
capitalize on their strengths and improve their weak-
nesses. Yet both managers and workers view performance appraisals negatively. Managers hate giving them;
workers hate getting them.

Management studies by the consulting firm of Kielty,
Goldsmith and Boone have overwhelmingly indicated
that feedback is one of the weakest links in management
practice. Managers avoid stepping forward with good
feedback; staff members are unreceptive to criticism.
Managers are reluctant to give criticism because they are
uncomfortable with the topic in general. They also resent
the time that it takes. Too often they choose to ignore a
problem with a staff member's work and hope it will
solve itself.

But if you were the staff member whose work was in
question, would you rather be informed that your work
is falling below expectations and discuss ways of improving your performance, or would you rather suddenly
get notice of a transfer, pay cut, or even termination?
When given that choice, I think we would all prefer to be
criticized.

When you are criticized on the job, examine the criticism carefully instead of reacting with one or another of
the Four Don'ts. Your critic could well be trying to solve a
problem or encouraging you to improve your perfor-

mance. We would all do well to take a tip from performing artists in this area. Timothy Nolan, an opera singer, says that good criticism is the best way for singers to advance their careers. "We hire people to criticize us," he says. It is impossible for singers to judge their own performance. They simply do not hear what the audience hears. Through vocal, musical, and language coaches, singers improve their skills. Without good feedback, many excellent singers would have remained merely mediocre.

✓ IMPROVE A RELATIONSHIP

Sometimes people criticize you to point out that your behavior is adversely affecting a relationship. If you want your personal and professional relationships to succeed and grow, you must pay attention and respond openly to this type of criticism. If you refuse to discuss the other person's perceptions and opinions about your behavior, then your lack of openness will likely lead to the deterioration of the relationship.

A good way to tell if a critic really intends to improve a relationship is the thoughtfulness of the criticism. Angry, arrogant accusations usually have some other intent behind them. If a critic is genuinely interested in improved relations and has exploded because of a need to vent feelings, he or she will return later to pursue the issue calmly and logically.

The critic will be willing and able to listen carefully to your responses and will display genuine openness. He or she will offer clear suggestions on how to improve. If your critic does not offer recommendations, then you should ask for them. This displays your openness to joining in to improve relations.

For example, Lillian has just criticized her husband, Rod, for lack of consideration. Rod examines the criticism and her delivery and decides Lillian is making a genuine attempt to improve their relationship. He asks her how he could be more considerate.

Lillian and Rod both work full-time, but she drives to

her job in their town and he commutes by train to a nearby city. She cites two or three specific instances when doing last-minute errands for him took her out of her way and cut into time she had set aside for going to the health club. She asks him to plan better, so that if he cannot take care of something himself and it is necessary for her to do it, she can do it without sacrificing her personal time. Rod promises to be more considerate in this way. Through Lillian's thoughtful criticism and Rod's openness to it, a small but nagging problem does not escalate and adversely affect a truly caring relationship.

This sounds like a storybook ending for Lillian and Rod, but it was arrived at only by a lot of diligence and hard work from both Lillian and Rod. Giving—and taking—thoughtful, constructive criticism takes time and effort.

On the job, congenial working relationships can be threatened for many reasons. One of the most common is an uneven distribution of work between equals, whether perceived or actual. Resentment can build unless the worker who believes that he or she is doing the majority of the work confronts the partner with a non-aggressive, well-thought-out criticism that includes suggestions on how to redistribute the work load.

Good criticism, and a receptivity to it, contributes to better working conditions and ultimately to getting the job done well.

✓ COMMUNICATE FEELINGS

If your behavior causes someone else to feel angry, hurt, frustrated or pressured, then a critical comment is necessary to let you know that.

A critical comment that intends to communicate feelings contains no name-calling or accusations. It is simply a statement that lets one person know where the other stands. It does not necessarily carry an expectation that the other person will change. Because intense feelings are often involved, it may be delivered strongly.

Here are some examples of criticisms given to convey feelings: "It's so frustrating to talk to you when you don't seem to be listening." "When you come home late without calling I feel angry and inconvenienced." "When you don't carry your share of the work load around here, I get ticked off."

Let's say a husband and wife are having an argument in the morning. The time comes when they must leave for work. "I get so mad when you say that," the wife says. "And I get angry when you do this," the husband replies. Then they put on their hats and coats and go to work. They have communicated their feelings and gotten rid of them. Pent-up feelings will not spoil their day.

If someone is honestly communicating his or her feelings to you, it makes sense to pay attention. Building strong relationships is tough if we don't know how our behavior affects others.

✓ *SHOW COMPASSION*

Offering criticism to help someone for whom a critic feels genuine empathy can help the other person solve his or her problem, pain, or discomfort. This is, however, one of the most difficult intents to decipher. Often this kind of critical remark can be construed as intrusive or controlling.

A good place to look for help in deciphering this intent is your knowledge of the other person. If you know a critic has your best interests at heart, then you should listen carefully to the criticism. If, however, in the past the critic has tried to control you or to see that things are done his or her way, then the intent may well be negative.

Kimberley, the account executive who has trouble on the job with her boss, Alex, was able to recognize the compassionate intent of an old boyfriend, now a good friend. When she was in the midst of a tumultuous relationship that was causing her a lot of pain, her friend criticized her pattern of becoming too dependent in intimate relationships. The criticism was carefully thought out and delivered kindly, so Kimberley was able to receive it and think about it. Because of her friend's criticism, she was able to recognize her pattern and understand why it did not help either her or her intimate relationships.

✓ PROTECT SELF-INTEREST

Critics must sometimes protect their own self-interest by criticizing you. They intend not to hurt or belittle you but to assert their own rights, including the right to hold their own opinions. This is perfectly reasonable, as long as it is not done at someone else's expense.

Let's take the case of Ralph and Florence. Both work full-time and equally share the indoor chores. Ralph, however, winds up doing the brunt of the yard and garden work. Florence does a few things in the garden but does not shoulder her share of the load. Ralph continually criticizes her for not helping him more outdoors. He does this not to nag or badger her but to assert his right not to be the unpaid family gardener. As with any positively motivated criticism, Ralph is careful not to be accusatory or inflammatory when he is delivering criticism to assert his rights.

✓ MOTIVATE YOU TO GROW

Loving people in your life often criticize you to steer you away from a destructive path or to help you grow. In fact, they have an obligation to do so. Your receptivity to this kind of criticism will, at least partly, determine your rate of growth.

As always, consider intent: it is in your best interests to determine if the critic is trying to help you grow or wants instead to assume a position of moral or intellectual superiority over you. It is important not to relinquish your individuality to satisfy someone else's need to be dominant. It is equally important not to cling so doggedly to our own ideas that we fail to take advantage of our critic's observations.

Years ago, I was developing a course for the management training division of a large corporation. The person who hired me made several suggestions regarding my presentation. It was clear from the way he made his criticisms that he was not trying to get me to teach the course his way. He was trying to make the course more compatible with the needs of the corporation. I made the necessary changes and was grateful to him. I am sure the success of my program was partly due to his comments.

WHEN NEGATIVE INTENT SEEMS POSITIVE

We have seen how easy it is to mistake positive intent for negative. But we must remember that the converse is also true. Criticism may appear to be aimed at improving our performance when, in fact, it is an attempt to control us. A critic may appear compassionate but may in fact be trying to manipulate. Again, it is vital to look beyond appearances and to search thoroughly before assigning an intent to a criticism.

Take Bernice, for example. Her job in middle management for a Midwest-based food company requires her to travel a great deal. She eats a lot of meals in restaurants and as a consequence has put on an extra twenty or so pounds. Bernice's mother frequently warns her daughter about the health consequences of being overweight and urges her to diet.

Bernice is well aware of her weight problem but for various reasons has decided not to give priority to it at the moment. She has told her mother this and requested that her mother stop urging her to diet. Yet her mother continues to bring up the subject of Bernice's weight. So Bernice has concluded that her mother's intent was not, as it seemed at first, to get her to improve herself. Her mother's criticisms were actually a ploy to control Bernice's behavior.

Because it is often difficult to decipher intent, it can be helpful to solicit outside feedback from thoughtful, well-informed people in arriving at your final determination. Despite the best of intentions, we can fool ourselves. If you consult others, remember it is to your best advantage to present the situation objectively. If you don't, you may end up fooling others as well as yourself, thus invalidating their response.

The motivations behind criticism are so often not what they seem to be at first. We must invest a good amount of time in unraveling the tangled threads of intent, and the time we spend sorting out our critic's motivations is always well spent. For without being sure of intent, it is difficult to choose the response that will allow us to deal successfully with criticism.

3

Preparing for Change

THE TECHNIQUES IN this book deal with your communication with others; they are *external* communications skills aimed at changing life-long habits. This is never an easy task. So before you begin learning the techniques, I want to talk about some vital *internal* communications skills that will help you learn and adopt these new habits.

As with any new skill, practice is key.

SETTING GOALS

Writing down your goals and monitoring your progress helps ensure that you will attain the outcome you desire. Thinking of your goal as "outcomes" rather than "achievements" sends a more positive message to your subconscious. You may not always reach a goal, but no matter what you do, you will always achieve an outcome. If it is not the one you desire, you simply adjust your strategy and try again.

Use the following guidelines to write out your desired outcomes in relation to criticism:

1. *Be specific*. If you write down *exactly* what you want, then you will know when you have achieved it. Choose both long-term and short-term goals and set a realistic time frame for achieving them. Make sure that your short-term goals will lead to the long-term

outcome you want. Break your goals down into tasks that you can do on a daily or weekly basis. Make a list of these tasks in order of priority. Check off each desired outcome as you achieve it. Be sure to congratulate yourself for successfully completing each task.

2. *State your outcome in positive terms and in the present tense, as if you have already achieved it:* "*I respond to criticism in an adult manner, feeling confident and in control of myself,*" rather than, "*I will stop responding to criticism in a childish way.*"

3. *Stay in control.* Make sure your outcome is something you can do directly. If you choose as an outcome changing someone else, that goal is out of your control; you cannot do it. You can change only yourself, not others. Your changed behavior may affect others, but it will not necessarily change them.

4. *Be realistic.* Set high expectations and standards for yourself, but do not choose an outcome that is totally out of reach. If you are fifty years old and your goal is to become the first female president of the United States when you have never had a job outside the home or participated in any political activity, you are in trouble. Stretch your mental and physical limits, but do not set your sights so high that you set yourself up to fail.

5. *Make a commitment.* Be sure the outcome you envision is one you truly want. If it is, commit yourself to it fully. Remember that determination is a key element in reaching your desired outcome.

The time you spend writing down your goals and monitoring your progress is likely to be less than the time you spend watching the evening news, yet it will have a much stronger and far-reaching effect on your life.

So get out a pen and notebook and write, right now.

CHANGING YOUR SELF-IMAGE

In *Birth and Death of Meaning*, Ernst Becke wrote, "Almost all of one's inner life when he is not absorbed in some active task is a traffic in images of self worth." To Becke's words, I add a few of my own: "And we can control, or guide, those images."

Our self-image, that subconscious picture we have of ourselves, is one of the determining factors in how we cope with criticism. A poor or weak self-image makes criticism difficult, sometimes impossible, to deal with.

We form our self-image over the years by our responses to experience, without our conscious thought or planning. Because of our self-image, we believe certain things about ourselves, and those beliefs lead us to behave in certain ways. A strong, positive self-image brings about strong, positive action. Self-doubt, on the other hand, makes our performance in life less than it could be.

The exciting thing about our self-image is that we don't have to accept the one we have right now. We can accept those parts of our self-image that satisfy us and reprogram the ones that don't.

Since the subconscious is incapable of differentiating between a real success and one that is vividly imagined time and time again, we can change our self-image by changing our beliefs. There are a number of techniques that enable us to do this. Among them are affirmation, visualization, and positive self-talk.

Affirmations are the words we live by, the phrases and sayings that automatically run through our minds and trigger our responses. Many of the words we live by are unfavorable and negative and create a negative self-image that harms our self-esteem. Replacing them with positive, upbeat messages is the first step in changing those parts of our self-image that make it difficult for us to cope with criticism.

Working from your list of goals, write a series of positive statements about yourself in relation to the way you handle criticism. Remember to phrase your goals in the present tense. If you write them in the future tense, they are apt to remain in your future. Here are some examples:

"I remain cool and confident when my boss criticizes my work."

"I respond in an adult manner when my mother criticizes the women I date."

Writing your affirmations on index cards and keeping them handy will enable you to refer to them throughout the day.

Each day, as often as you can, read each affirmation and *visualize* the outcome you want. As you vividly picture yourself in the circumstances you desire, let yourself feel the pleasurable emotions that accompany the attainment of your goal.

Remember that your subconscious does not know the difference between an actual experience and one that is vividly imagined. You can change your inner picture of yourself. When you do, your behavior will change as well.

At the same time that you are working on your *affirmations* and *visualizations*, try to become more aware of your internal monologue, your *self-talk.* Notice the way you talk to yourself, and notice how often what you say is negative. When you catch that little voice inside you saying, "I can't handle it when Carla puts me down in meetings," switch that voice off. Change the tape. Tell yourself, "I know exactly how to handle Carla when she tries to put me down in meetings."

Here are some affirmations you may want to work into your self-talk. Actually say these things aloud and repeat them inwardly from time to time:

"I learn from criticism."

"I accept criticism."

"I remain strong and in control when I am criticized."

"I use criticism to my advantage; therefore, I welcome it."

"I can't wait to be criticized."

"I have learned and am learning how to use criticism to build my self-esteem and sense of personal power."

BRINGING FEELINGS INTO BALANCE WITH THINKING

In ordinary circumstances, our thoughts and feelings remain in relatively good balance. Criticism, however, often causes our feelings to completely overshadow and undermine our thinking. It is essential that you learn to bring your feelings and thinking back into balance before considering or answering a criticism. If you try to apply the coping techniques when you are hot and bothered, you will probably not be very successful.

Fred had worked hard on his proposals for a major marketing campaign for his firm. He went into the meeting where he was to present his proposals feeling confident and well prepared. If we were to diagram the balance between Fred's thoughts and feelings it might look something like this:

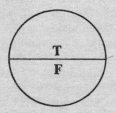

About five minutes into his twenty-minute presentation, Fred's immediate supervisor viciously attacked one of Fred's recommendations. The attack threw him off balance and aroused his already negative feelings about his supervisor. He became angry, anxious, and noticeably flustered. His feelings became so strong he virtually stopped thinking and could not answer the questions his attacker was firing at him.

Fred's thoughts and feelings looked something like this now:

In this instance Fred lost his cool entirely and stumbled through the rest of his presentation. There are, however, a number of things Fred could have said to give himself time to regain his composure. Where is it written that he is required to respond to an attack or challenge immediately? Here are some sample responses that will gain valuable time to get thinking and feelings back into balance:

"Let me think about what you've said and I'll come back to it later."

"I'd like to take a few minutes to think about that. How about a ten-minute coffee break?"

"I'd like to think about what you've said and talk to you about it later." (This tactic moves the confrontation out of the public arena and lessens the pressure on you. The other participants will probably be relieved, too.)

The technique of asking for time can be used in any situation where you are being criticized, not just on-the-job meetings. If you sense your thoughts becoming overpowered, it is perfectly reasonable to request a moment to think about what your critic has said.

Another way to restore balance between your thinking and your feelings is to vent the feelings. This is a very personal process, and you will need to find the way that suits you best.

For me, it is saying a four-letter word. I can do a lot of venting with one four-letter word, uttered to myself in public or out loud when I am alone.

Here are some other venting tools. Obviously, you must choose ways of venting that work for you and are appropriate for the time and place: pace; talk to a friend; go into a closet and scream; slam a door; write it down; take three deep breaths.

Many people ask, "But if I vent my feelings in the closet all the time, how will anyone know that I have any?" Honest and timely expression of feelings is one of the elements of good relationships. But you don't want to knock people over the head with your emotions. You merely want the other person to know where you stand.

I am not suggesting that you lose your feelings or become too careful or guarded with them, but do learn when and how to vent with other people so that your feelings don't get the better of you—or the relationship.

You can say things like, "I'm really angry right now. Let's talk about this later." Or, "I'm so angry now that I know I'll say something I'll regret. Let's talk about it when I've cooled down some." If both you and your critic are operating with a full head of steam, you'll probably end up engaged in a good fight, saying thoughtless things you may regret later.

You can't cope with criticism or solve the problem that gave rise to the criticism when the steam is pouring out of your ears. You must first bring your feelings back into balance with your thinking. Then you and your critic can have a useful discussion.

In some cases, especially intimate relationships, your feelings may be easily and often aroused. Take the time to communicate rationally. If you frequently find that is not possible, seek the help of a professional or third party who can help you stand back a little.

SUPPORT

A support system can be very helpful as you work to change your life-long responses to criticism. Having someone to talk to will reinforce your progress and help keep you from lapsing back into your old behavior patterns. You may ask a friend or colleague for half an hour of their time each week to discuss your progress. Or, if you know a number of people who want to restructure their responses to criticism, you may want to form a support group.

Here are some brief guidelines for setting up a support group. These suggestions follow the model in *Developing Support Groups: A Manual for Facilitators & Participants* by Barbara Glaser and Howard Kirshenbaum (University Associates).

1. Schedule meetings at a convenient time and place to facilitate participation.
2. Based on the amount of time available, assign each participant a set period of time to talk to the group. This should be at least five minutes per person.
3. Participants may ask the group to do one or two of the following during their presentation: simply listen; ask clarifying questions; offer suggestions; offer support between meetings.

   This structure will keep meetings running smoothly and ensure that all participants have a chance to speak and to get feedback.

   Participants should be reminded that each person comes into the group with different levels of awareness, ability, and dedication. Each person progresses at his or her own pace. It is important that participants measure improvement in relation to themselves and not in relation to others. Competition among group members should be discouraged.

BELIEVING IN SUCCESS

If you believe in success, you will be empowered to achieve it. If you believe in failure, then you will surely fail. So, write the word failure out of your vocabulary. If something happens, and it is not the outcome you wanted, then look it over carefully and see what lesson you have learned from that outcome. Adjust your plan of action and move on.

It is important not to wait for evidence to embrace the belief that you can deal with criticism and use it to empower you. If you wait for evidence that you can succeed, you may end up waiting a long time. If, however, you practice and apply the skills in this book, no matter what you currently believe, you undoubtedly will learn to deal successfully with criticism.

PART TWO

How Words Work

4

Silent Observation and Careful Listening

SILENT OBSERVATION IS the first skill you must culti-
vate in order to develop successful strategies for dealing
with criticism. The silence I am about to describe is very
different from the kind where you withdraw to seethe
silently or plot revenge or justify your actions. This other
kind of silence is a conscious choice on your part, not a
habitual, unthinking response. It is something you decide
to do to remain in control when you are being criticized.

Silent observation allows you to distance yourself
from criticism; it gives you time to get your thoughts and
feelings into balance; it helps you gain the objectivity
and need to decipher intent. If you do not immediately
lock yourself into a particular response, you will be less
likely to respond instinctively with one or another of the
Four Don'ts. You will begin to find that more choices are
available to you, and you will come to better understand
yourself and your critic.

AN EXERCISE IN SILENT OBSERVATION

✓   *STEP 1*
First, give yourself permission not to respond to criticism. Make a conscious decision to remain silent when

you are criticized and to concentrate on sheer observation.

For the next week—or longer if that is what you need—listen carefully to the criticism around you and especially to the criticisms aimed at you. (Focusing on criticisms leveled at others as well as the ones you receive enables you to practice an objective stance. You will also learn from noticing how others respond to their critics.)

Do not respond to your critics, except perhaps to say something like, "I'll think over what you said." You may wish to not say anything at all but instead acknowledge the criticism with a nod or some other nonverbal, noncommittal sign that you have heard your critic. If the criticism comes in the form of ridicule or a put-down, you may wish to make no acknowledgment at all.

✓   STEP 2

During the week, think about the criticisms as you observe them. Ask yourself these questions:

What is the critic's intent?
How do I feel about the criticism?
Do my feelings get in the way of using the criticism?
How do I want to respond initially?
How would I respond after some thought?
Is there any validity in the criticism? How much?
How might I have wasted the valid part of the criticism if I had reacted right away?

At the end of the week, ask yourself:

How have my feelings changed with silent observation?
Have I been able to distance myself from criticism?

Have I been able to learn and increase my understanding of criticism by silently observing? If so,
what have I learned?

✓ *STEP 3*

Use affirmations to reinforce your conscious decision
to remain silent and observe. Here are some phrases you
may want to incorporate into your self-talk:

"I am remaining silent and calm in order to listen
carefully."

"Silence creates the opportunity for me to learn."

"In my silence I am becoming more secure; I am in
control of my behavior."

"Silence is a great alternative to the Four Don'ts, and
it's so easy."

This exercise is sure to empower you where criticism
is concerned. By not letting yourself get hooked you will
deepen your understanding of criticism. With clarity and
objectivity you will begin to change your thought process and create the psychological space you need to
learn the rest of the skills.

Here are some examples of how silent observation
created the opportunity for scrutiny and thought:

Anna and George. After twenty-one years of reacting
defensively or changing her behavior to stop George's
criticism, Anna made the decision to remain silent and
observe. This was the first step in changing her behavior
when George criticized her.

Silence allowed Anna to zero in on George's intent.
After several weeks of observation she concluded that
George was not trying to hurt or abuse her. He was
overly directive because he wanted the world to run his
way. Anna also realized during this period that by trying

to please George and do everything his way, she had allowed her self-esteem to become badly eroded.

With her new understanding, Anna was ready to break the pattern of those many years with George and learn to deal with his criticism on an adult-to-adult basis.

Kimberley. Kimberley gave silence a try after eight months of reacting immediately to her boss Alex's criticisms. Instead of following her usual pattern of defending herself or arguing, she gave herself permission not to respond immediately when Alex criticized her. The feelings of being worthless and out of control that she had previously experienced began to lessen.

With her thinking more in balance with her feelings, Kimberley was able to realize that her own insecurity led her to argue or defend herself with Alex. She needed to prove to him that she was right as much as he needed to prove he was boss. Once she recognized and released that need in herself, she found herself much better able to cope with Alex's criticism.

Not only did her ability to remain silent help her feel stronger, but Alex began to criticize her less and less. Now that he wasn't getting a rise out of her with his critical comments, he was less apt to criticize her. Her negative feelings towards Alex began to change, and their working relationship improved.

In the course of silent observation you may notice that some criticism is without merit. Once you have carefully examined the criticism and your feelings about it, you may decide that your best choice is to say or do nothing further.

Letting a criticism go can be very difficult. Pay attention to your self-talk, making sure not to put down your critic or yourself. Also, make sure that by ignoring the criticism you are not building up an inventory of unhealthy emotions. If you choose to continue to ignore the criticism, you will need to vent any anger, frustration, or resentment that may build up. You may want to go into a closet and scream, or you may find it helpful simply to smile and say to yourself, "There we go again." People in public life respond this way a great deal. How many times have you seen a public figure answer a critical question or remark with, "No comment."

To silently ignore a criticism is sometimes the best way to deal with it. But you must be sure you are not really withdrawing to silently seethe or try to get even. When you withdraw you are denying your real feelings about the criticism. Silently ignoring a criticism should empower you; if it does not, then it is not the best way to deal with the criticism.

Becoming a good silent observer means learning to listen. True listening is one of the most difficult communications skills to master. It takes a great deal of discipline to listen well, for you must set aside your own prejudices, frames of reference, and desires in order to enter the speaker's world.

Yet listening is critical in order to learn from criticism. Only when you really listen to someone can you hear what they are saying. Only by listening can you make a genuine connection with another person. And only then can you begin to know that other person, for you will have begun to hear what lies behind his or her conscious intent.

Listening takes intense concentration and single-mindedness. You must focus only on the speaker. You must forget yourself completely—what you think and what you want to say. This is not an easy task, but the rewards are great. I recall a friend happily telling me not long ago, "You know, I've been listening to my son for

years, but it wasn't until today that I really heard what
he was saying." There was a look of pure joy on his face
as he spoke. He had truly listened; he was elated.

When you really listen, you not only come to know
another person but you learn about yourself as well. Putting aside everything—defensiveness, distracting self-
talk, plans for a counterattack—allows you to absorb
what the other person is saying without distorting it for
your own purposes. You can hear what they are saying
and use those words to your own benefit. Really hearing
someone else's true meaning can be a significant contribution to your own self-discovery.

By listening well to criticism, you open the floodgates
to good, sound information about the way others see
you. Whether or not you ultimately decide that you
agree with your critic's perceptions, listening gives you
the opportunity to learn. You do not lose the benefit of
useful, instructive criticism by refusing to listen to any
criticism at all.

If listening is so rewarding and worthwhile, then why
are we generally so bad at it? A number of things get in
the way.

Preoccupation with making our own point. Begin to pay
attention to the frequency with which you find yourself preparing your response as the other person is
speaking. When you do this, you cannot possibly hear
what is really being said. Consequently, your response may be what you want to say, but it doesn't
address the issue at hand.

Distracting, irrelevant thoughts. Thoughts constantly
scurry in and out of our consciousness. You may be at
a meeting about a new sales strategy, but instead of
concentrating on the sales manager's presentation,
you are thinking, "I wonder if it's going to rain today,"

or, "I'm chilly," or, "Isn't he ever going to shut up? I want to get my say in, too."

Deciding we already know what the other person is going to say. We think much more quickly than we can speak. If we are not truly listening, our thoughts are moving all over the place while someone else is talking. Frequently they jump ahead to second-guess the speaker. Have you ever stopped someone in mid-sentence to say, "I know just what you are going to say." Well, guess what? You don't know.

Carl Rogers, in *A Way of Being* (Houghton Mifflin Co., Boston, 1980), laments: "What I really dislike in myself is not being able to hear the other person because I am so sure in advance of what he is about to say, that I don't listen. It is only afterward that I realize that I have heard what I have already decided he is saying; I have failed really to listen."

Twisting the speaker's message to fit our expectations. We often listen selectively, distorting the speaker's words to fit our perceptions not only of what we want to hear but of who the speaker is. Once again, Carl Rogers: "Just by twisting his words a small amount, by distorting his meaning just a little, I can make it appear that he is not only saying the thing I want to hear, but he is the person I want him to be."

If we think of the speaker as an ogre, we will hear a hateful, malevolent message. If the speaker is an angel to us, we will hear a heavenly choir. Neither of these may be the case, but because we have not heard the speaker's real message, we can continue to hear what we want.

ROADBLOCKS TO GOOD LISTENING

Let's look at some of the specific behaviors that prevent us from being good listeners. Make a conscious effort to notice when you and others set up these roadblocks. The more aware you are of these behaviors, the more you will catch yourself before falling into the trap.

Interrupting. Any interruption, even a clarifying question or a suggestion, diverts the speaker's attention and stops the flow of thoughts and feelings.

Identifying. "That very same thing happened to me just a year ago." The speaker does not want to hear about your past problems; he wants to talk about the current issue.

Ordering/Directing. "You go and apologize to her." Nine times out of ten, the proposed action is what *you* would do, and does not necessarily help the speaker.

Warning. "If you don't take care of this right away, you're going to have trouble on your hands." Dire predictions do not increase anyone's understanding of a particular issue.

Advice/Suggestions. Watch out for the words "should" and "ought." If the speaker wants parental-type advice, he or she will ask for it.

Lecturing. "Now, I've had a lot of experience in this matter, and I really think you should..." No matter how much experience you've had, you do not know what is right for another person. What you did in a similar situation is not necessarily what someone else should do. Offering information could indeed shed some light on the topic. When the speaker has finished talking, you can make a statement about what you have observed in your life, but do not assume that it is applicable to his situation.

Interpreting. "What you really mean by that is..." The speaker has told you what he or she means. Why try to change it?

Diagnosing. "You're only saying that because you're upset." Let the speaker do any diagnosing. If a speaker asks you for analysis, that is one thing. Otherwise, don't second-guess.

Expressing Impatience. "What are you trying to say?" Directing a speaker to get to the point will not help. This is especially true if the speaker is trying to express feelings. Demanding instant clarity says in effect, "I am not interested in listening to you until you have carefully formulated your ideas." It also discourages the speaker from future discussion of feelings with you.

Criticizing/Disagreeing. "You are not thinking straight," or, "You didn't handle that well at all." Comments like these can shut a speaker down, even when they are your honest interpretation of the situation. A speaker in the process of venting feelings is not interested in—or ready to take in—feedback.

Probing/Questioning. "Why did you say that?" or, "Charlie? You mean the guy who drives the brown Volvo?" Asking questions like these can throw the speaker off the track. If you want to ask a question merely to satisfy your own curiosity, then wait. Questioning can be an extremely effective tool for helping another person dig deep for solutions, but questions that sidetrack the speaker are not good aids to listening.

Patronizing/Praising. "Don't worry about a thing. You've got what it takes to make it all work out." Even though praise is important in all relationships, it can be a roadblock to good listening. A speaker who is venting strong feelings needs to keep going and will not welcome this kind of interruption. Misplaced praise, especially when it seems to play down the other person's feelings, can appear patronizing.

Telling the Person What to Feel. "You shouldn't feel so angry. He didn't mean anything by it." Be careful not to assign emotions to the speaker. Just listen to the expression of feelings.

Reassuring/Consoling. "You'll feel better later," or, "Things aren't as bad as they look." Being supportive and consoling is beneficial at times, but if you are busy patting the speaker on the back, you will not hear what is being said. Wait until the speaker is finished. Then it might be appropriate to offer reassurance or consolation.

Offering Distractions/Joking. "Let's go get a cup of coffee. That'll take your mind off it," or, "You think you've got troubles? Just the other day I heard about a guy who . . ." The story that follows that lead-in could be true or it could be a joke; in either case the intention is to get the speaker's mind off the problem. But heading someone off from talking is not being a good listener. Even if you succeed in diverting the speaker's attention, the unexpressed feelings or problem still remains.

Even though many of these roadblock behaviors are helpful in the proper context, they serve as a deterrent to good listening if they are used at the wrong time. One of the trickiest parts of being a good listener is timing, sensing what kind of listening the speaker requires at any given moment.

For instance, if my husband has had a frustrating day with one of his big customers, he might come home wanting to blow off steam. Or he might come home wanting me to suggest some alternatives for solving his problem. If I offer suggestions when what he really wants is a silent, attentive ear, then I haven't been listening to him very well.

He may not know exactly what he wants when he walks in the door and starts talking. But if I do not meet his needs, he may say to me: "I don't want to know what you think right now. Just listen, please." If I wasn't really listening to him I might not hear his request that I switch gears. Even if I truly believe I have the answer to his problems, I keep my thoughts to myself until he expresses a need to hear them. One of the most caring and loving things you can do in any listening situation is to put aside your own desire to offer an opinion until the other person is ready to receive it.

TECHNIQUES FOR CAREFUL LISTENING

✓ *SILENCE*

You cannot talk and listen effectively at the same time. You cannot plan what you are going to say—that is, talk to yourself—and listen effectively at the same time. Only by your attentive silence do you respect what the other person is saying. When you interrupt, look away, or otherwise remove your attention from them, you are telling the speaker that what is being said is not important or interesting or worthy. If you truly wish to listen, pay attention and remain silent.

Hold your silence for a few seconds after the other person has finished speaking. Then you can collect your thoughts and decide on your response. But while the other person is speaking you must hang on every word. Make a contract with yourself that you will do this. As soon as you make a conscious decision to be silent and listen, you will find yourself interrupting less, your attention will wander less, and you will hear more of what the speaker has to say.

✓ *ACKNOWLEDGMENTS*

Few things are more irritating to speakers than to see a listener staring off into space or doing something else. The speaker is expending a lot of thought and energy to tell you something; the least you can do is offer your undivided attention for a few moments. If you can't take the time to listen at the particular moment when the speaker wants you to, say so. Don't waste the speaker's time—or your own.

It is difficult to allow your eyes to wander and truly

listen at the same time. Therefore, if you acknowledge the speaker by maintaining eye contact, you will have a much better chance of understanding what is being communicated.

Also, be aware of your body language. Are you physically open to the speaker? Or have you turned your body to the side with your legs crossed and arms folded? Put your pencil down and push away anything else you might be tempted to fiddle with. These objects only come between you and the speaker.

Another way of acknowledging the speaker without breaking silence is to nod occasionally when appropriate. With silence, eye contact, an open body position, and a few nods you can communicate to the speaker that you are really listening.

✓ DOOR-OPENERS

We communicate by many means besides the spoken word: the look in our eyes, our facial expression, body position, sighs, or groans. If by any of these signs you notice that someone is upset but reluctant to talk, you may want to take the initiative and open the door for more overt communication.

Opening doors is a skill that needs especially careful cultivation by people who are in a position of power, as parent, teacher, department head, chief executive. No matter how conscientious you are about responding openly to feedback, there will be times when your response is defensive, impatient, or short-tempered. This is likely to discourage the less powerful from communicating with you honestly. Therefore, to encourage continued feedback, you must constantly be on the lookout for signs of discontent. When you have time, carefully open the door and listen.

It is always a good idea to get things out in the open.

In business, unspoken criticism about performance 〈
decisions can undermine operating procedures and affect
professional relationships. In personal relationships, unspoken criticisms tend to build resentment, undercut intimacy, and affect the physical and emotional well-being
of the person who is keeping them in. Good listening
starts with noticing and acknowledging signs of trouble.

Door-openers are simple statements like:

> "You seem down. Want to talk about it?"
> "Something on your mind?"
> "You look sad. What's going on?"
> "You seem confused. Want to sort something out?"

Another way of opening the door is simply to be
there. If you're aware that someone is having a tough
time, you might offer your presence as support and give
the other person the opportunity to start a conversation.
You might suggest a simple, relaxing activity, like taking
a walk or having a cup of coffee, that will provide an
opening. It isn't necessary to question or prod. Allow the
other person to move at his or her own pace. Don't im-
pose your timetable. Your open, receptive presence may
be enough.

It is easier to offer an attentive ear to someone whose
problem does not concern you than it is to open the door
for discussion with someone who is upset with you. To
initiate communication when you may be on the receiving end of some sharp criticism or strong negative feelings, you must have the capacity to go outside yourself
and become completely absorbed in what the other person has to say. This takes courage and a great deal of
awareness and patience.

But the more you make these overtures, the more
sensitive your antennae will become. By picking up signs

...y have upset someone you will be able to nip ... painful situations in the bud. It's like exercis- ...long-unused muscle: the more you use it, the stronger it becomes.

When Beverly and her children went to spend Thanksgiving with her sister Sandra, Beverly noticed that Sandra avoided eye contact and lacked her usual warmth. The sisters lived hundreds of miles apart, but they exchanged visits a couple of times a year and attended larger family gatherings as well.

Initially, Beverly simply spent time with Sandra to give her an opportunity to talk. She suspected Sandra was still hurt as a result of a misunderstanding that had occurred during a family reunion the previous Christmas. But Sandra did not say anything about that or about anything else. Finally, Beverly gently opened the door. "The last couple of times we've been together, you've seemed distant or preoccupied. Is there something you'd like to talk about?"

Sandra took a deep breath and let Beverly have it. Apparently, Sandra had felt unwelcome at Beverly's house the last time she and her children visited. Sandra gave several instances of how she and her kids had felt they were imposing on Beverly and her family. Beverly listened carefully, despite the fact that it was difficult to hear some of the things Sandra had to say. When Sandra was finished, Beverly, in a non-defensive way, explained that the visit had come at a time when she was preoccupied with an important project at her job. She had thought about asking Sandra to postpone the visit, but didn't want to disappoint her or the children. Because Beverly was brave enough to open herself up to her sister, the two women were able to discuss the problem and restore their previously warm and close relationship.

Remember that not all non-verbal communication is a

sign that someone is in trouble or is upset with you for some reason. Some manipulative people use non-verbal communication to get attention or produce guilt.

Jenny often complained that her son Tom, a doctor, did not spend enough time with her. In her telephone calls to Tom, Jenny would frequently sigh or moan or groan. She gave these signals to manipulate Tom; they were Tom's cue to ask what was wrong. Tom had to learn not to respond only to his mother's spoken words and not to her manipulative signals. If she made an outright request of him, he would respond to it, but he ignored the sighs and groans that were nothing more than oblique hints. In time, Jenny gave up what had clearly become a futile tactic.

So, do strive to become aware of non-verbal communication. By all means, respond to someone's genuine distress or discontent, but do not give up your own control by responding to non-verbal communication that is meant to manipulate you.

✓ QUESTIONING

Once the door has been opened and the speaker has said his or her piece and vented whatever emotions he or she needed to vent, well-phrased questions can help the speaker focus more clearly on the problem at hand. Good questions are non-inflammatory; they elicit specific information that will help the speaker gain perspective. Poorly phrased questions may discourage the speaker from saying anything further. Avoid questions that implicitly criticize the speaker's actions: "Why did you do it that way?" or, "Didn't you think about the consequences?"

Harvey had just taken over his father's business. His father had run the business largely on instinct, but Harvey was a professionally trained manager and was taking a more systematic approach. He noticed, however, that many of the older employees seemed distant and unfriendly to him. He approached Mark, a man whose opinion he respected.

Mark responded to Harvey's door-opener by telling Harvey he was too "business-like" and making changes too fast. It was difficult to get used to the new way of doing things, Mark said. Harvey acknowledged that his management style was different from his father's, and then asked Mark if he disagreed with any of the new policies. It turned out that Mark agreed with the policies, but not with the way they had been presented. Harvey asked Mark to suggest ways of presenting the new policies more effectively.

Through this exchange Harvey gained a better understanding of why his employees were not satisfied, and he was able to take steps to alleviate that dissatisfaction. Mark was able to vent his feelings and anxieties about the changes in the business and learned that his opinion was still valued by the new boss. The outcome was obviously favorable to both men.

✓   *PARAPHRASING*

When you paraphrase, you repeat back to the speaker the essence of her communication in your own words. You do not interpret the speaker's statements or give your opinion of them. You merely restate the speaker's exact meaning.

Paraphrasing forces you to listen well. You must pay attention to every word the speaker says if you are to be able to repeat it. I do not mean that you should try to memorize the speaker's words and repeat them verbatim. When you paraphrase, you want to show that you have understood and processed the communication. This conveys to the speaker your genuine interest in and commitment to understanding what has been said.

Paraphrasing is particularly useful when you find your mind wandering. If you focus on understanding the communication so well that you can repeat it in your own words, you will pay better attention. It is also a good technique to use when you are not absolutely certain you have received the speaker's message. If your paraphrasing is not right on the money, the speaker will be able to tell you so.

The moment I ask workshop participants to paraphrase what I am saying, a sense of quiet and attention comes over the room. People lean forward in their seats with looks of marked concentration on their faces. As soon as I point this out they understand the power of this important listening skill.

After asking participants to paraphrase what I have said, I divide the group into pairs so that they can practice the skill with one another. The noise level in the room is much lower than for other verbal exercises. Because the listeners are concentrating on the speakers' meaning and are not preoccupied with their own responses, interpretations, or opinions, they interrupt much less often. And because the speakers have a sense of being listened to, they tend not to speak so loud.

You need not paraphrase every single point that comes up in the course of a conversation. If you did that, conversations would take a very long time. But you might want to paraphrase mentally most of what the speaker says. Then, from time to time, paraphrase orally.

I remember a manager who commented to me after the paraphrasing exercise, "So that's what Phil has been doing. There's a guy who does a lot of paraphrasing at our bi-monthly staff meetings. I could never figure out exactly why he was doing it, and in a way, I always thought it was a pain in the neck. But I know he never fails to deliver exactly what he's been asked for. Because he checks and rechecks his assignments in the course of the meeting. It's his way of ensuring that he knows exactly what we want. Come to think of it, I admire him for it."

✓ *REFLECTIVE LISTENING*

In reflective listening you make a statement to a speaker—after he or she has finished speaking—about your impression of his or her feelings. In other words, you reflect back to the speaker the feelings you have discerned beneath the spoken words.

Greg, a teenager, comes home from playing soccer for the school team and asks his mother in an aggrieved tone, "What's for dinner? When are we eating?"

Mom can respond to the words only and give the information requested: "We're having broiled chicken and we're eating at seven o'clock." Or she can respond to what she believes are the feelings behind Greg's words: "It's broiled chicken at seven. You seem really upset tonight."

The second answer invites Greg to say more about his feelings. Mom has also shown that she is tuned in to him and that she is trying to understand him.

Be sure not to make judgments or recommendations about the other person and remember to speak in a neutral tone of voice.

For instance, Mom shouldn't say, in a sharp tone, "Greg, you're really upset tonight. Go take a hot shower and calm down." If she does, she has assigned her son a feeling he may or may not have and she has shown impatience with his mood. Assigning feelings and impatience are both roadblocks to good listening.

Encouraging someone to speak through reflective listening can be difficult if the speaker is criticizing you. If you can stay calm and in control, the speaker will have let off some steam and will probably feel better. And, by allowing him the free expression of his feelings, you have communicated your openness.

We all have feelings, and there is no point in challenging someone else's feelings or telling the other person "not to feel that way." Making a neutral observation about the other person's feelings is, however, a good way to invite someone to open up, to give him or her room. It isn't necessary to be "right" in your statement of what the other person is feeling. Merely making your honest observation is often enough to open the door.

Let's pursue the conversation between Greg and Mom.

Greg stalks into the kitchen, slams his bookbag down on the table and asks, "What's for dinner, Mom? When are we eating?"

Mom takes a moment to silently observe Greg. "It's broiled chicken at seven. You seem really upset tonight."

"Mom, you hardly ever go to my soccer games."

Mom's other commitments prevent her from attending many games. She and Greg have talked about this before, but she does not remind him of that. She continues her reflective listening. "I guess you're pretty angry with me."

"No, I'm not really angry," Greg admits.

"Well, maybe you're disappointed that I can't make every game."

"Yeah, I am disappointed."

By responding to her son's anger personally, Mom was able to allow Greg to vent his feelings about her non-attendance at his soccer games. They went on to talk again about why Mom can't make every game, and she then promised to attend a game that was particularly important for Greg's team. Greg released his resentment about his mother's not coming to the games, which had built up even though he understood intellectually that his mother could not be there every time. For her part, Mom showed an openness and willingness to accept Greg's feelings, even though she knew she could not change her availability for the games. She did not berate him for "feeling that way" nor did she tell him he "should" have understood that she could not be available to him whenever he wanted her to be.

It is important when listening reflectively not to question and probe. Deep probing when someone is being carried on the wave of his emotions can halt communication. Reflective listening is meant to enable the other person to express feelings, not to get him or her to examine and analyze them.

Reflective listening is an important skill for anyone who has to handle complaints on the job. Complainants are often irrational and full of emotion. Yelling helps them to get out their strong feelings, even if the person they are yelling at cannot fix their problem. Workers and managers who find themselves on the receiving end of complaints will do everyone involved a service if they can learn not to take the shouting personally. Then they provide complainants a mechanism for getting rid of their anger and frustration, after which everyone concerned can get on with solving the problem.

A school superintendent once told me that reflective listening turned around what had been arduous school board meetings. He found that if he simply allowed irate parents the floor for a few minutes to vent their feelings, and if he openly acknowledged their anger and frustration, they would soon run down. Then all participants were able to engage in a more rational give-and-take discussion.

"Allowing them their feelings is key," he said. "I may not be able to change the fact that their child has to wait in the cold or the rain for the school bus, but I can recognize that this is troublesome and worrying. That makes all the difference in the world." And, a bonus to him, reflective listening made the school superintendent feel less defensive and more in control of these meetings.

Since silent observation and careful listening are crucial in learning to deal with criticism, I suggest you make a real commitment to acquiring these skills. Affirmations will help you considerably to honor this commitment. Tell yourself in the morning and the evening and a few times during the day, "I am a good observer and a good listener. I truly value observing and listening. I am getting better at these skills every day."

When you are listening, it is important to set yourself aside and totally accept the other person no matter what he or she is saying. Sensitive, accurate, non-judgmental listening enriches any relationship. You will feel pleased when you are successful in truly listening to another person; you will also feel disappointed when you find you have not listened well. When you realize you've fallen short of your goal, simply resolve to do better the next time.

Silent observation and careful listening will lead you to greater knowledge and deeper understanding of the communications and transactions that govern a critical dialogue. A period of silence and listening will aid you immeasurably in deciphering the intent of your critics and in choosing the most suitable technique for handling any critical situation.

5

Defusing Criticism

DEFUSING IS A technique for shaking off negatively motivated, destructive, or cruel criticism. You offer no resistance, but you do not let the criticism penetrate; you do not allow your critic to hit the mark; you take the bite out of critical comments that are not intended to help you grow.

Picture a large bomb with a long fuse. If the bomb explodes, it means that a negative criticism has been successfully delivered to you. The fuse is lit and burning fast, but you pull it out before the bomb can explode. And the negative criticism has done no damage.

This is how defusing can protect you. It can take the punch and power out of the annoying, sarcastic, snide remarks that have hooked you for so many years.

Defusing is probably the most powerful skill you can use to unlearn your defensive behavior. Daily digs and picky, meaningless criticisms—often delivered by loved ones—frequently elicit defensiveness. Making a conscious effort to defuse them will get you off the defensive merry-go-round.

As I've said, before responding to any criticism it is important to decipher intent. Deciphering intent is particularly important if you are going to defuse. Defusing is a powerful means of putting a stop to unwanted critical comments, so if you defuse a criticism that is positively motivated, you will halt communication between you and your critic and deprive yourself of the benefit of that criticism.

EXERCISE PREPARING TO DEFUSE

✓ *PREPARE TO DEFUSE*

Before you start to defuse, take a week to observe silently. During that week keep two running lists of the negative criticisms you observe. One list should contain criticisms leveled at you; the other should note criticisms delivered to those around you.

Pay particular attention to judgment words in the criticisms. Words like passive, stupid, lazy, demanding, selfish, aggressive, disorganized, etc. These words do not reflect reality. Behavior reflects reality. Subjective words reflect the speaker's opinion, nothing more. Just because someone interprets a particular behavior as bad or wrong—and this can be inferred from the speaker's tone of voice as well as his words—does not make it bad or wrong. That is simply one person's opinion. Taking a ten-minute break does not make you lazy; it means you are taking a ten-minute breather. Running late does not make you disorganized; you are just running late on that particular day.

Making these lists will accomplish two things. First, it will heighten your awareness of the criticism around you. Perhaps you have been listening to critical remarks without being fully aware of how they are undermining your self-esteem. Or perhaps when you really listen to what people are saying you notice that you sometimes say similar things and put people down without realizing it.

Second, as you observe and make your lists you will find that your feelings are no longer so easily triggered by criticism. The process of observing and noting allows you to objectify and distance yourself. You will be thinking more and feeling less. This is one way of overcoming the negative emotions attached to criticism. When you overcome negative emotions, you will be more in control.

Through your observations, you will become aware of many things you never saw before. Perhaps you will see that some people are more critical than others or that constant nagging remarks you tended to slough off are wearing away at your positive self-image as surely as tiny drops of water ultimately wear down a rock. Every piece of knowledge you collect will increase your understanding and help you develop your skills.

Next, divide your lists into three columns. In the lefthand column, write down the key critical word or words of a transaction. In the center column, note the behavior that elicited the criticism. In the righthand column, list the positive qualities that you or others attribute to the behavior.

For example, Vince tells his wife, Lucy, that she is selfish for choosing to spend the evening at a meeting about local zoning regulations rather than staying home with him and the children. Lucy sees her decision as an opportunity to learn and to be of service to her community. This is what Lucy wrote on her list:

Key Critical Words	Behavior	How I or Others See It
selfish	went to meeting	learning, community service

Be sure to remember as you make your lists that the purpose of this exercise is not to exonerate yourself (or the person you have seen criticized) or to justify a particular behavior. You are creating a tool to help you get out from under negative criticism.

If you notice when you make your list that you have heard the same criticism from a number of different people, then do sit up and pay attention. Your critics could have a point, and you may need to consider the behavior that elicited the criticism rather than defusing the criticism you receive.

WAYS OF DEFUSING

There are several different tactics for defusing criticism. You can:

✓ *AGREE WITH PART OF THE CRITICISM*
There is often some truth in what is being said.

Criticism: "I see you're wearing that old-fashioned tie again."
Response: "Yup, I'm wearing that tie again."

Criticism: "I see you're going for a run this morning before you even do the dishes."
Response: "Yes, I am."

Some years ago I conducted an assertiveness-training program for nurse-educators in a southern city. Word soon got out that a northerner with some "pernicious" ideas had descended upon the hospital. On more than one occasion I was stopped by a doctor and asked something like, "Are you that aggressive woman from New York here to teach our nurses how to be aggressive?" My response was, "I'm that woman from New York."

Before the week was out, I was able to overcome a lot of the resistance I encountered in the hospital from doctors and administrators. I'll talk more about this experience in later chapters, but suffice it to say for now that defusing helped me stay in control during that difficult first day or two. After that, I was able to use the more interactive techniques to communicate with people who had reservations about what I was doing. By not rising to the bait when a snide comment came my way, I was able to get my critics to take me seriously and eventually listen objectively to what I had to say.

Defusing is an excellent way to stay in an adult position when someone continues to criticize you just to prove a point, even after you've discussed the matter. Take Doris and Hank. Doris is busy professionally and asks Hank and their children to help her around the house. Hank reluctantly helps out, but he thinks Doris is too fastidious in the way she does some household chores.

After fluffing the clothes in the dryer, Doris hangs the wash on the line. The clothes do not wrinkle or shrink so much, and she likes the fresh smell of line-dried clothes. Hank thinks that if Doris spent less time hanging the wash on the line, she wouldn't have to ask him and the children to help so much. He frequently makes critical comments:

"I see you're hanging the clothes on the line again."

"Yes, Hank, I am."

"Are you sure you have the time?"

Doris continues calmly with her task. "Looks like it."

"We sure do have our priorities."

"We sure do."

Doris chooses to defuse Hank's remarks because she knows that Hank is not trying to improve her or their relationship. He just wants to prove that hanging out the wash is stupid. By defusing, Doris does not have to be continually explaining why she chooses to take the time to hang out the wash.

But let's say Doris does not defuse Hank's criticism about hanging the wash on the line. Instead, she defends herself and feels childish. What if she lets Hank's remarks wear her down? She then acquiesces and does the wash his way. But every morning, when she dresses or hugs her children before they go off to school, she is reminded that she just doesn't like the feel or smell of clothes dried in the dryer. Resentment, even anger, builds about doing the wash "Hank's way," even though she made the choice. When critical intent is negative, defusing can head off a lot of trouble.

If, however, Doris examined Hank's intent and decided he was trying to help her, then defusing would not be a good choice for dealing with his comments. In an intimate relationship, when the other person is criticizing you for positive motives, defusing can create distance and mask real problems. Once again, the challenge is to decipher the intent.

✓ *AGREE WITH THE POSSIBILITY THAT YOUR CRITIC COULD BE RIGHT*

Without changing your own opinion or behavior, you stop your critic in his or her tracks.

Every time you take a break, a certain co-worker accuses you of goofing off. If you defuse, you can slide out from under those sarcastic remarks.

Criticism: "So, I see you're goofing off again."
Response: "It looks that way, doesn't it?"
"If you don't straighten up, you could lose your job."
"You could be right. If I goof off I could lose my job."

Here's another case. A co-worker challenges a detail of your unfinished proposal:

Criticism: "Your evidence is not substantial enough. It'll never work."
Response: "You could be right, but let's proceed and decide about that after the final proposal is made."

This is an exchange between a husband who knows that his wife often uses criticism to manipulate him:

Wife: "You know you exercise too much. If you don't watch out you'll wind up in the hospital with a heart attack."

Husband (recognizing that his wife is using this ploy to get him to sit in the sun with her): "You could be right," he says as he hops on his bicycle.

✓ *RECOGNIZE THAT YOUR CRITIC HAS AN OPINION*

From his or her perspective, what your critic says is true:

Criticism: "Running is such a dumb, destructive activity. Why do you keep doing it?"

Response (as you lace up your shoes and lope out the door): "I know it seems dumb to you."

Criticism: "I can't understand why you spend so much time with Sue. She's a real bore."

Response: "I guess she is to you."

Criticism: "Your decision to buy from that supplier is ridiculous. You won't get good service."

Response: "I can see why you'd say that."

In this last example, perhaps your critic did have difficulty with the supplier in question. But you might also be aware that the difficulty was caused by a personality conflict that has nothing to do with you. You don't have to bring up what might have been a distressing experience for your colleague, nor do you have to get sucked into defending your position. Defusing allows you to follow through on what you believe is a good decision for you without belittling your critic or getting defensive.

✓ *RECOGNIZE THAT THERE ARE OTHER OPTIONS*

This does not mean you will embrace them.

Criticism: "Running is a stupid activity. You'll end up permanently damaging your joints."

Response (as you finish your pre-run stretching and head out the door): "I suppose I could swim."

Criticism: "That dress is frumpy and the color doesn't suit you."

Response (this is your favorite dress): "I have other dresses that you probably like better."

Criticism: "Your dresser drawers are a mess. You really should tidy them up."

Response: "I suppose I should."

Criticism: "If you had half a brain in your head, you'd approach the project this way..."

Response: "I suppose I would."

✓ *AGREE WITH OBSERVATIONS OR DESCRIPTION OF BEHAVIOR, BUT NOT WITH IMPLIED OR OVERT JUDGMENTS*

The tone of your critic's voice is an indicator of implied judgments. A demeaning or stern tone means that the critic is talking down to you and is implying that you have made a mistake or failed. We all know what that tone of voice sounds like—we heard it often enough from our parents when we were children. Imagine that tone in the delivery of these implied judgments.

Criticism: "There are three empty boxes taking up all the space in the cupboard."

Response: "So there are."

Criticism: "You sure have trouble getting moving in the morning."

Response: "I sure do."

Overt judgments are also handled well by defusing.

Criticism: "Our ten-year-old can shovel the walk more thoroughly than you can."

Response: "He shovels snow very well."

Criticism: "Our division gets final figures a lot quicker than yours."
Response: "Your division is quick all right."

Criticism: "It took you a day and a half to finish painting that small bathroom. You sure are disorganized."
Response: "Yes, it did take a day and a half."

Deep sighs and groans can imply judgment just as well as tone of voice. You will do well to ignore these non-verbal criticisms and respond only to the spoken word.

✓ *USE HUMOR*
Humor is an extremely effective way of defusing. You can nip a put-down in the bud and lighten things up at the same time. Be sure not to use sarcasm though. That is counterattack, not defusing.

Criticism: "You men sure are rotten listeners. You need to take a few lessons from us women."
Response: "What did you say?" or, "Eh?"

Poking fun at yourself can lighten things up, too.

Criticism: "Hey, guys, you'd better talk real slowly and clearly. Buddy's here. He doesn't get things the first time around."
Buddy: "Yup, take it nice and easy, fellas."

Criticism: "Are you sure you had your eyes open when you were pitching today?"
Response: "I had one of them open."

EXERCISE IN DEFUSING

Once you have spent at least a week observing and listing criticisms around you, you are ready to put into practice what you have learned about defusing.

✓ **STEP 1**

Make a list of critics with negative intents. List who criticizes you, what they criticize you about, your critics' intents, your responses to and feelings about their criticisms. The list you made of criticisms directed at you for the preparing to defuse exercise will be useful here.

Note which critics give you thoughtless and/or destructive criticisms. Take a moment to think about the intent of these critics. On close inspection, are you certain their intent is negative?

When you are sure about who is criticizing you with negative intent, take a blank piece of paper and make a list of those critics whom you think it would be useful to defuse. Also note their most frequent criticism(s) of you. Take your time. Be as objective as you can.

✓ **STEP 2**

Write defusing responses. Plan and write down as many defusing responses as you can think of for each of your critics. Writing down your responses is an effective way of collecting your thoughts; it also allows you to re-read your possible responses and become comfortable with them.

The people on your list may be close to you, and anticipating dealing with their critical behavior could well make you uneasy. This is perfectly natural. It may help to say to yourself something like, "I feel a little uncomfortable, but I am handling my emotions. I'm feeling more comfortable every minute. Soon I will feel fine. I know this works."

✓ **STEP 3**

Picture yourself delivering your defusing responses. Relax in a place where you will not be disturbed. Picture a scenario in which one of your critics is criticizing you.

When you have finished, go on to the next one on your list.

If you want to have some fun with this part of the exercise, picture your critic in his or her underwear. This is especially helpful if you have endowed your critic with undeserved power and status.

Another plus of this device is that it helps you lighten things up a bit. You may have some anxiety about this exercise, and humor is an excellent way of relieving it. At times, it's a good idea not to take life too seriously.

Now, visualize the exchange between you and your critic, using the defusing responses you have just written. Hear the words that your critic says. Then hear yourself defusing each criticism. Feel yourself staying calm and in control. Hear yourself speaking steadily and confidently. Enjoy the sense of achievement that is rightfully yours after you have defused the criticism. Be sure to smile and feel the joy of success. This sends a strong, positive message to your subconscious.

✓   *STEP 4*

Write your affirmations. Affirmations will reinforce the power of your imagined scenarios. Here are some examples:

"I love to defuse unimportant/destructive/negative criticism. It feels so good, and I'm good at it."

"I'm getting better and better at defusing every day."

"Defusing really works. I can do it and I feel strong and powerful."

"I am ready to defuse. I know how to go about it."

"Defusing is meant to empower me, to help me take charge. It does not belittle the other person."

Choose any of these affirmations or create your own. Just be sure that each is stated in the present and in a positive way. Repeat your affirmations several times a day or whenever you need them. Keeping them handy on index cards is helpful.

✓   *STEP 5*

Do it! Pick the person on the list in whom you have the least emotional investment. This might be a co-worker or casual acquaintance, a friend, or even a member of your family, but it should be someone you are ready to approach. The next time that person criticizes you, *defuse*.

Of course, it may not be possible to start with the easiest person. You may not run into him or her for two or three weeks. Don't let that hold you back. You have prepared, visualized, and written affirmations for all your critics. Seize as many opportunities as you can to put your hard work to good use.

As you gain practice and experience, move up from defusing those critics in whom you have the least emotional investment to those in whom you have the most emotional investment.

The defusing technique will bring you one of two possible outcomes. One, you will be successful. Your critic will be silenced and you will feel terrific. If that happens, pat yourself on the back, praise yourself, and enjoy your achievement.

Two, you may stammer or struggle. Your critic may persist and silence you. If that happens, run the episode through your mind and ask yourself, "What have I learned?" Think about what you will do differently in your next encounter with this critic.

One good thing about not meeting a goal is that it gives us the opportunity to learn. When things don't go according to plan, we can adjust and try again. Be sure, however, to keep your self-talk positive and productive when you make a mistake. Tell yourself, "I'm learning from this," or "I'll get it next time."

Don't give in to the urge to run after your critic and launch into a lengthy explanation after you have successfully defused. Your old patterns of behavior are deeply ingrained. You may not be able to change them all the first time you try. But each time you try, you have learned something. You are sure to succeed if you keep trying and believe you can attain the outcome you desire.

One of my first successful experiences with using the defusing technique was about ten years ago, at a point in my life when I would have gone to the head of the class in defensiveness. I had just learned the defusing technique and was incorporating it into my life.

At that time I lived in a small ski town in the Adirondacks. My sister and her children had planned to visit for a skiing holiday during a week when school was in session for my kids. Because I thought it was important for my sons to spend time with their aunt and cousins, I decided to take them out of school for a couple of days. I discussed this decision with their teachers and school administrators. All agreed that the boys were doing just fine. They could see no reason why my children shouldn't spend a few days with visiting relatives. I felt I had done everything a responsible parent needed to do in that circumstance.

But there was a neighbor who didn't think so. His name was Ted, and he was known around town as the local put-down artist. He threw me a wiseguy line almost every time I saw him, and every time I bit the hook. I defended myself against his barbs, then was furious with myself. I had planned to practice the defusing technique on Ted. I had written out my planned responses and imagined myself delivering them. I was ready and committed to success.

The second day that my children were skiing with their cousins, Ted skied up beside me at the top of the mountain. He said, "You've got those children out of school *again*?"

"Yup," I answered.

"Boy, Mary Lynne, you sure are a nonconformist."

"I've been told that before."

I had defused Ted's comments twice; I was still calm

and in control and I thought maybe he'd ski away. But he wasn't about to give up.

"Listen," he continued, "if you don't watch out, those kids could turn out to be juvenile delinquents."

I was getting a little hot now. Who was he to tell me how to raise my kids? But I stayed cool and kept on defusing. "One or two of them could."

"I can see it all now. They're going to go to the end of town, steal a car, drive by your house and you'll shout, 'Have you got enough gas?'"

"I wouldn't want them to run out of gas in a getaway car."

With that, Ted turned and skied away. There was a part of me that wanted to ski after him and explain all the reasons why I took the kids out of school and how I had cleared it with their teachers and that I am a wonderful, responsible mother who bakes whole-wheat bread every other day.

But I didn't ski after Ted, and within thirty seconds I felt great. I had really taken charge.

That experience was a turning point for me. Once I'd had that success, I kept using the defusing technique and getting better and better. Up until then, my success with defusing had been hit or miss. But when Ted skied away I realized how much I had learned from my mistakes. I kept trying, and one day it worked just the way I had been practicing in my visualizations. Today, ten years later, defusing is as available to me as defense used to be.

Of course, there are times when I forget and defend or counterattack in response to a criticism. This sometimes happens with people I am close to who catch me off guard. Other times, it happens in threatening professional situations. But now I am aware of my lapses, which are fewer and further between than they were even a couple of years ago. I still, however, continue to learn from my lapses.

An added bonus to my successful defusing of Ted was

that our relationship improved. After a couple more attempts to bait me, which I defused, he stopped trying. I'm no longer annoyed at him for being a smart aleck, so I don't avoid him, and he treats me with a new respect. Ted is only an acquaintance, so his snide remarks were a relatively minor annoyance to me. But being able to defuse those remarks gave me so much confidence that I was able to move ahead and practice defusing on critics with whom I had much stronger emotional ties.

Is defusing a put-down? No. When you are defusing, you never call your critic names; you never make judgments about what was said; you never deliver a defusing response in an aggressive, overbearing manner. If you do any of these things, you have counterattacked. But if you keep your tone neutral and your attitude quiet, calm, and non-threatening as you respond, you have defused.

Why should you continue to be a victim of people who attack you with negative intent? Defusing robs your critics of their anticipated outcome. Instead of enhancing them at your own expense, you have enhanced and empowered yourself. There is nothing wrong in maintaining your self-interest and self-esteem in the face of a critic. Defusing merely affords you a way of doing this.

When you are defusing a criticism, even though the words you choose may be light and humorous, you are not engaging in banter, because the criticism offered was not so intended. In banter, both (or all) participants are equally entertained and satisfied by the exchange. But once one participant becomes harsh and tries to score points at the expense of others, then the exchange no longer qualifies as recreational banter that all are enjoying equally.

Of course banter can relax a difficult situation. Remember Laura, the head nurse, and the doctor who was called on her shift? Let's rewrite that critical exchange.

The doctor enters the nurse's station and collapses on Laura's chair. "We've got to stop these midnight rendezvous. They're killing me. I can't remember the last time I had a full night's sleep."

"You're not supposed to get a full night's sleep. You're a resident."

"And I suppose you're here to see that I don't?"

"I sure am. It's one of the first things they teach us in nursing school."

Both Laura and the doctor enjoyed their verbal Ping-Pong game. There was no implied criticism in his remark about her being the one responsible for disturbing his sleep. And she took none. Both of them perform stressful jobs, and a little lighthearted banter helps get them through the long nights. If, however, the doctor had started to make comments that were intended to put him one up on Laura, she would have been perfectly justified in defusing him.

CASE HISTORIES

Let's return to the case histories introduced in Chapter 2 and see how defusing works as a response to negative intent.

✓ DOMINATE / CONTROL

After twenty-one years in a marriage in which her husband, George, has sought to dominate and control her through criticism, Anna has come to realize that in order to stay in the relationship, she must realign the balance of power between them. She and George are currently engaged in a struggle over Anna's exercise program. Here is a conversation that is typical of the way Anna and George relate to one another:

"Anna, I have just the exercise plan for you. You've always had difficulty with your weight and there's no reason why you shouldn't get on a strict exercise program. I've made all the arrangements for you to join the daily aerobics class at the Y. All you have to do is go down and sign in and you'll be all set."

Anna has already decided to walk and run with some of the women from her support group, and she has signed up for tennis lessons. "George, I've decided on an exercise program of my own."

"You never stick to anything, Anna. You've tried lots of different things over the years and you always drop out in a few weeks. These classes are structured; that'll make you stay with it."

"I have stuck to things from time to time, and I know right now my plan is going to work for me."

"You haven't stuck to a thing yet. You're still over-weight. You talk about exercising, but you don't do it."

"But I am going to do it this time, George. I promise I am."

"Promises don't amount to a hill of beans, Anna. It's action that counts."

After this final barb Anna was speechless, and she felt awful. At the next support group meeting she reported the encounter. I asked her what she had learned. She looked crushed and almost tearful. "You see," she exclaimed. "I even forgot to tell myself to think about what I learned when I didn't do well with George."

Anna's defensiveness had put her in the position of a child during the confrontation. Then she amplified her mistake with her negative self-talk. She had already completed a period of silent observation and careful listening during which she had realized that George knew exactly how to hit her where it hurt most. When we analyzed this recent confrontation, she saw that she had let George do just that. Then we talked about how defusing could help her, even if she felt awkward when using it at first. I then suggested that she practice defusing; I would take George's role.

"Anna, you are overweight and you don't follow through on any of your exercise programs, so I've enrolled you in a structured aerobics program."

"You could be right, but I'll choose my own program."

"That won't work. You never follow through on things, Anna."

"That could be."

"Well, then, I'll plan it for you."

"No, I'll do it myself, George."

"But you just said that you don't follow through on things."

"Yes, I did say that."

Through this role-playing exercise, Anna saw that it was possible for her to defuse George successfully. She understood that although her husband knows where to aim his arrows she doesn't have to let them hurt her. She could use defusing as a kind of total body shield that would deflect George's arrows and keep them from harming her. She declared herself ready to try the technique on George himself.

Anna came to our next meeting beaming. George had brought up the exercise program three times over the week. Although she had been nervous and stammered her first defusing responses, she continued to focus on the technique and not on the feelings she was experiencing. This helped her get over the feelings. By the third encounter, she had become a defusing expert. From that time on, Anna became better and better at defusing. Naturally, she had a few setbacks, but she was able to learn from them.

Defusing helped Anna the most by getting her out of the defensive, childish, powerless stance she had so long taken with George. Once she was in a more equitable position she was able to think clearly about the problem. First of all, she recognized that George tried to dominate and control everyone. She was not inadequate, as he frequently told her she was. This was his way of staying in a dominant position. Over the years he had reinforced the insecurities she brought to the marriage, and she had colluded with him by acquiescing and assuming a powerless position. George's forcefulness, persistence, and sharp tongue did not make him right; they just made him a more powerful speaker. Anna also realized that although her husband spoke forcefully, his listening skills were underdeveloped and underused.

Besides objectifying and distancing herself through the silent observation and careful listening she had done, Anna worked on modifying her self-talk and writing out her goals. Her long-term goal was a relationship with George in which they were complete equals. Her short-term goal was to defuse all of George's criticisms. Over the next several months she practiced defusing and was successful a great deal of the time. Anna was finally able to get off the parent/child merry-go-round she and George had been riding for so long. The more she defused, the more autonomous, in control, and, yes, even powerful, she felt. As she gained stature in her own eyes —and in George's—she was ready to move on to the more interactive skills.

✓   *MANIPULATION*

Defusing is a great way to get a critic to stop trying to instill guilt. Your critics learn that they can't push your buttons and give up trying to manipulate you.

Tom, the busy doctor and family man who lives three hundred miles away from Jenny, his mother, was tired of explaining to her that he had a lot of demands on his time. He was also tired of her manipulative ploys, both verbal and non-verbal. Tom was especially distressed by Jenny's constant comparisons of him with Bruce, the son of a friend of hers. Their relationship was becoming very draining—and time-consuming—for Tom. Defusing, however, helped Tom to stop getting hooked by Jenny's manipulative ways.

Tom was well aware when his mother's birthday was, but he had a medical conference to attend that weekend. When he told Jenny, she said, "Bruce took his mother to the beach for a whole week to celebrate her birthday. Bruce really loves his mother."

Tom could see the worm wiggling on Jenny's hook, but still didn't bite. He remembered to deal with his mother's words, not her implied judgment, so he said,

"Bruce really does love his mother. That's nice."

"So you won't have time to get away next month and visit your mother on her birthday."

"You're right. I'm going to be busy."

"Well, you do have your priorities."

"Yes, there are things I really have to do." Tom resisted the urge to defend himself by explaining why it was important that he attend his medical conference.

"I have only one birthday a year, and you don't even have time to come to see me then."

"I'm sorry it's worked out this way, but I have to be out of town."

"A good son would try to be with his mother on her birthday."

"No argument. When I can, I like being with you for special occasions." Again, Tom replied to what Jenny said, not to her implication that he was not a good son.

Defusing put Tom in control of himself in his relationship with his mother. He was able to deal with her on an adult level, not to slip back into being what he once was, her defensive child.

✓ *PUNISH / GET EVEN*

Bill and Mary have an ongoing conflict about how much time Bill spends at home. Despite discussions, Mary persists in getting her digs in about Bill's spending too much time away from home. Frequently, she does this in public, which makes it even harder for Bill to respond. I have seen Bill get hooked a number of times.

"Bill is never home," Mary will say.

Bill blushes and defends himself. "I'm home a great deal, Mary. I'm working long hours, but we do have part of Saturday and all day Sunday together."

"Not last weekend. You worked all day Saturday and part of Sunday morning, too."

Bill gets redder in the face. "That was only last weekend. That was unusual."

"Oh, yeah," Mary says sarcastically.

Defusing gave Bill an alternate way of coping with Mary's repeated criticisms on this topic, especially when there were other people around.

When Mary makes a remark like, "Bill is never home," Bill can respond with "I know it appears that way at times."

Or there was the time when another couple asked if Bill and Mary wanted to attend a concert with them the following week.

"Well, we'll see if Bill will stop working long enough."

The pre-defusing Bill might have said, "Oh, come on, Mary. That's not fair. You know I'll go to the concert."

But now that he knew how to defuse he could answer with, "I know you have your doubts about getting me out of the office, Mary, but let's get the tickets anyway."

I know that Mary and Bill have a good, loving relationship, and that they have talked about this a lot. But Mary still tries to punish Bill because he is not doing what she wants, spending as much time at home as she would like him to.

In close relationships where there are small disagreements that surface despite previous discussions, try this:

1. State your position clearly and engage in a good, fair give-and-take discussion of the problem. Make certain your partner understands your position. This may solve the problem. If, however, your partner continues to criticize you from time to time, move on to step 2.
2. In the face of continued criticism, objectify. Don't let your feelings take over.
3. Defuse.

There is no need to allow yourself to be punished when you have been direct and honest with your partner. Defusing will keep you from becoming a victim of punishing remarks.

✓ *ABUSE*

In an abusively critical relationship, defusing allows you to detach yourself from your critic, a crucial outcome if you are to salvage your self-esteem.

Many spouses of alcoholics have told me that defusing absolutely saved their sanity. Alcoholics (and other substance-abusers) can be extremely abusive with their criticism, especially if they have not faced up to their problem.

Karen is married to an alcoholic. For years she was worn down by his abusive criticism and nearly lost all vestiges of self-esteem. Now that she has learned to defuse, her self-esteem is returning, and she has been able to bring a modicum of peace to her household. She has considered leaving the relationship, but she wants to leave from a position of strength, not run away as a weak, powerless victim.

By defusing, she has been able to detach herself from the ugly, vicious remarks her husband makes when he is drunk. "Defusing is the best single skill I have for holding on to my self-esteem in this marriage," she told me.

Although Bob is not an alcoholic, Margaret, too, has been worn down by her husband's venomous outbursts and is fighting hard to regain her self-esteem and assertiveness. She wants to give the relationship a chance to improve, but she has not been able to get Bob to take a look at the part he is playing in their problems or to engage in rational discussions of them. She is reluctant to leave because of their baby daughter. Like Karen, if she does decide to leave the relationship she wants to walk away with her head held high.

Margaret's experience with defusing has been valuable. Though she is not yet happy in her marriage, she is happier with herself and the progress she has made in reclaiming her self-esteem and sense of personal power. As she has become more skilled in defusing Bob and learning from her mistakes, she has been able to enjoy the present more. She can love the kind Bob and detach herself from the hostile, abusive Bob.

Here are some of Margaret's successful defusings:

Bob: "This house is a mess. The baby's toys are all over the place and the hamper is overflowing. You're a slob."

Margaret: "It looks that way, doesn't it?"

Before she learned to defuse, Margaret might have tried to defend herself by telling Bob how hard she had worked on an article she was writing and then how she had taken the baby out to the park to enjoy the beautiful day, so she didn't have time to tidy up. But Margaret had learned that the more she defended herself, the more abusive Bob became. By depriving him of the apparent pleasure he took in hurting her, she was able to stem his attacks somewhat.

One evening Margaret was out doing an interview for an article and did not arrive home before Bob. Bob found the baby with a sitter and no dinner on the table. The minute she walked in Bob attacked her: "You're never here when I get home from work. Then you work on the weekends, too. You leave the baby with a sitter too much. And there's never anything to eat around here. You sure don't know how to be a wife or a mother."

Knowing she had a defusing response ready, Margaret was able to stay in control of her emotions: "I'm sure there are plenty of women who are better at it."

She had no need to counterattack by saying something like, "I wouldn't exactly call you the best husband in the world. You're not helpful and you're very moody." Nor did she defend herself by explaining where she had been, how important her work was, how well she really did take care of the baby, or how fitting in household chores around her work made it necessary sometimes to do the marketing or other errands in the evenings. Bob may have continued his tirade, but Margaret did not let herself fall prey to it.

✔ *PROJECT / TRANSER*

Even when Margaret was in the very frustrating position of hearing Bob criticize her for the undesirable characteristics she observed in him, she was able to defuse and disregard his critical comments. She was careful to deliver her defusing comments with a show of little interest or emotion. This was a clear indication that she would not respond to Bob's goading.

"You know, you are really self-centered, Margaret."
"I know I probably appear that way to you, Bob."

Or, "Margaret, you don't know the first thing about how to be a loving spouse."
"Perhaps I don't."

Margaret learned to have a number of defusing responses ready, so that she could call on one any time she needed to.

✔ *SLICE*

Defusing easily takes the zing out of the potshots that slicers like to deliver. Cynthia, the computer scientist who had trouble with a slicing co-worker, caught on to the technique right away when it was presented in the workshop she attended. Cynthia's self-esteem and confidence were good. She simply needed a concrete way of dealing with Stan's constant slicing.

Stan: "I can't stand it when you make statements you
    can't back up."
Cynthia: "I'm sure you can't."

Stan: "I wouldn't go in there and ask for a raise if I were
    you. You can't talk your way out of a paper bag."
Cynthia: "You could be right."

Stan: "A woman could never figure out that problem."
Cynthia: "I can see why you would say something like that."

Cynthia was certain to make these comments in a neutral, offhand way. Soon Stan's slices were rolling off her back like water off a duck.

✓ *GET ATTENTION*

Attention-seekers want the spotlight to shine on them. If you defuse, you automatically deflect the light away from them. This is what Jonathan, the corporate manager, did with Herb, who challenged him with constant plays for attention.

At a meeting, Herb broke in on Jonathan's presentation. "What are you talking about? I don't see how your group is going to accomplish that in only a month."

Jonathan responded mildly, "I'm sure you don't." And he continued with his proposal.

But Herb butted in again. "Hold on. You're not being clear. Explain to me how you're going to do it," he demanded.

"It may not be clear to you right now. If I haven't answered your questions by the time I've finished making my pitch, why don't we talk about it in my office later?"

In the cafeteria one day, the group was talking about football and Jonathan cited a statistic he'd read in the Sunday paper. "That's nonsense," Herb challenged. "Where did you get a statistic like that?"

"I suppose it does seem like nonsense to you," Jonathan replied and went back to what he had been saying.

Jonathan had been successfully defusing for a month when Herb said, "Boy, Jonathan, you're easy to rile. You rise to the bait every time."

"Whatever you say, Herb."

In a sarcastic singsong, Herb came back with, "Whatever you say; whatever you say; whatever you say."

Jonathan walked away smiling. Because of his success in defusing Herb's attention-getting maneuvers, Herb was getting frustrated. Herb was persistent and continued to try to "get" Jonathan. But defusing became second nature to Jonathan and allowed him to keep Herb out of the limelight.

✓ *CHANGE YOU*

Sometimes a critic's attempt to change you can be well motivated, so it's a good idea not to defuse these comments before you have examined them carefully. The criticism may have some merit. If it does not, however, a discussion about the matter might clear things up. Point out to your critic (who may not realize what he or she has been doing) specific instances that have been attempts to change you. Your critic may then promise to stop the behavior but may slip back into the old pattern from time to time. Then it's a good idea to defuse.

The problem with Tony and Jane however, wasn't so easy to resolve. Jane continued to try to remold her husband, criticizing everything from his clothes to the way he conducted himself professionally and socially. For a while, Tony acquiesced in Jane's demands, but he realized the toll this was taking on him. Ultimately, Tony was unsuccessful in saving their marriage, but he used defusing to stop Jane from totally undermining his self-esteem.

Jane: "Your clothes are so boring and conservative. It's time you wore something more exciting."

Tony: "I'm sure I look boring and conservative to you."

Jane: "Don't you care how you look? Your clothes are really horrible."

Tony: "Perhaps they are."

Jane: "Then let's get rid of them and get you some new ones."

Tony: "I'm going to keep these clothes."

Jane: "You should mix more at parties. You don't know how to get around socially."

Tony: "I'm sure it appears that way to you."

Jane: "You're never going to move up in your organization if you don't become more gregarious."

Tony: "You might have a point."

To hold on to your autonomy when a critic is making a concerted effort to change you, it is important not only to defuse their critical statements, but also to continue behaving in whatever manner is comfortable and right for you. Tony didn't learn not only to defuse Jane's attempts to change him, but also discarded the flashy clothes they'd bought and resumed wearing the clothes he preferred.

✓ *SHOW YOU WHO'S BOSS*

Although Kimberley knew perfectly well that Alex was her boss, he had a constant need to prove it again and again. He called her to task for every little thing. She learned to defuse Alex's nit-picking remarks and was able to maintain her own self-respect as a competent professional.

If you work for someone like Alex, defusing will be a very useful skill. Here's how Kimberley dealt with Alex when his criticism was meant only to demonstrate his seniority:

Alex: "Don't you think it should be done this way?"

Kimberley: "It could be done that way."

She might weigh Alex's suggestion later, but she would not react at that moment in any other way except to defuse, because Alex was not trying to improve her performance; he was showing her who's boss.

✓ *GET YOU OFF THE TRACK*

Attempts to get you off the track often occur when you find it necessary to deliver a criticism yourself. Even though your criticism was positively motivated, the other person may respond by becoming a critic.

When Jim moved into a managerial job, he found his former co-worker Steve resented his attempts to improve Steve's job performance. Jim learned to defuse and Steve was no longer able to throw him off the track.

Steve: "Now that you're the manager, you sure are giving me a hard time."

Jim: "It looks that way, doesn't it?"

Steve: "You're getting pretty uppity."

Jim: "I'm sure that's the way you see it, Steve."

Steve: "You used to do that, too, when we were working together."

Jim: "Maybe I did."

These defusing responses allowed Jim to follow through on his task—getting Steve to perform up to department standards.

✓ *UNDERMINE*

Defusing works wonders when someone is trying to undermine you. It puts you in a position of power, where your critic's remarks cannot diminish your status. Remember Rita, the executive who was being undermined by her colleague, Sally? Sally took every opportunity to cut Rita down, sometimes so subtly that Rita didn't even realize what was going on. Other times, Sally left Rita speechless. When Rita finally did catch on to Sally's tricks, however, she used the defusing technique to good effect.

Sally (ever so sweetly): "We know this isn't your strong point, Rita."

Rita: "That could be."

Sally (seemingly jovial): "Sweetheart, in that suit you could hop on any plane and get a free ride clear across the country."

Rita: "Good idea. I think I'll give it a try."

Defusing gives you a way of taking a clear stand with a sniper. If you allow someone like Sally to silence you, then she knows she's scored. The other thing Rita remembered to do was to wear that suit again and make sure Sally saw her wearing it. She refused to give Sally power over her by shoving it to the back of her closet.

✓   *VENT FEELINGS*

When someone vents feelings on you, you can defuse or you can listen reflectively. Reflective listening will help your critic vent and get rid of uncomfortable feelings, but there will be times when you haven't the time or the patience to listen or help. At those times, defuse the remark. In neither case should you take the criticism on. Positive self-talk will help you keep your own feelings in balance.

Criticism: "This place is a junk heap. The garage is so crowded with hockey sticks and bikes and basketballs, I can't even get in it."

Reflective response: "Rough day today?"

Defusing response: "Things are pretty messy, aren't they?"

When Fran, the line manager, examined her boss's frequent outbursts, she realized Martin was probably under pressure from above. Still there was no reason she should be burned just because Martin needed to blow off steam. She learned to defuse.

Martin: "This work area is a wreck. I've never seen it look so bad."

Fran: "It could look better."

Martin: "Can't you motivate your crew? It's only 9:30 in the morning and they're behind already."

Fran: "They have had better days."

✓ *GET ONE'S OWN WAY*

Giving in to people with short fuses is a sure way to reinforce their unrealistic view that the world revolves around them. When you collude in letting them have their own way, you encourage them to continue in their spoiled, explosive behavior. Defusing is one technique that can put a cap on the volcano.

Sarah's husband Larry had a very short fuse, especially where "peace and quiet" were concerned. Her husband's demands were spoiling her and her children's ability to feel at home in their own house. Sarah began to defuse instead of giving in to Larry's unreasonable expectations.

Larry: "I don't want a bunch of kids traipsing through this house all the time. This is not a teen club."

Sarah: "No, this isn't a teen club."

A few days later her children were entertaining a few friends. Larry exploded.

"There are a bunch of kids down in the basement. Are you aware of that, Sarah?"

"Yes, I am."

"I thought I said this wasn't a teen club."

"You did say that. Your kids are just having a few friends over."

"A few friends! It sounds like a rip-roaring party."

"I recognize it may sound that way to you, Larry, but it's just a few friends."

When dealing with short fuses, you must be careful to take a position and stick to it. State your limits, and tell your short fuse what you want. You will have to repeat your position time and time again, for short fuses are not used to limits.

Defusing is useful when you do not want to discuss or confront a problem that has already been discussed. Sarah had talked to Larry about the fact that she believed their children had a right to have their friends in the house regardless of Larry's position on "peace and quiet." She had pointed out to him that she and the children had as much right to enjoy their home as he did.

Now she sticks to her position, defusing his still-frequent outbursts.

Larry: "You want everything your own way, don't you?"
Sarah: "It looks that way, doesn't it?"
Larry: "I'm nothing but a wage earner around here."
Sarah: "It's too bad you see it that way, Larry."

It takes patience and persistence to deal with short fuses, but unless you want to live life their way, you must use defusing and the other techniques to keep them from walking all over you.

✓ *GET A LAUGH*

Defusing takes the sting out of toxic humor without making an issue of it. There are circumstances in which it is possible to initiate a serious discussion about the grave effects of toxic humor, but in many situations such an attempt would backfire.

For instance, a man makes a sarcastic comment about women in a meeting. The one woman in the room indicates her strong dislike of such comments. The rest of the men rise to their colleague's defense, accusing the woman of not having a sense of humor or being too serious or trying to pick a fight. In a situation like that, it would be far more effective for the woman to make a defusing response.

Man: "We all know how hard you women are working to catch up with the guys, so let's see what you've done this month."

Woman: "We do work hard."

Man: "You ladies have to stay on your toes to keep up with us."

Woman: "We're on our toes, all right."

A humorous defusing response can counterbalance a joke made at your expense. Everyone has a good time, and it's a great alternative to getting a laugh at someone else's expense.

Comment: "Did you get a load of Benny's tie today? He must have bought it at the circus."

Response: "It's amazing what you can find at circuses these days," or, "Glad you like it."

Comment: "That car you're driving is the pits. You'd do better shopping at the junkyard."

Response: "Next time I'm in the market for a car, I'll try the junkyard. Thanks for the tip."

Defusing your critics may make you uncomfortable at first, but you will soon lose your awkwardness when you see how useful the technique can be. It makes you stronger, puts you in an adult position, and discourages negative-intent criticism. It is intended to distance you from your critics, so that you stop the criticism and the damage it is doing to you. It does not invite further discussion.

For this reason, defusing is not always the best technique to choose, especially in close personal relationships or important work-related relationships. In those cases, you want to improve communication as well as hold on to your self-esteem. You want to encourage adult-to-adult dialogues to get to the root of the problem. Genuine inquiry, the next technique we will study, allows for deeper investigation and leads to resolution of difficult issues.

6

Genuine Inquiry

GENUINE INQUIRY CLARIFIES criticism by questioning your critic. The choice of genuine inquiry over defusing depends on what you want to accomplish. If you want more information about the criticism, if you want your critic to think about what he or she is saying, or if you want time to think and pursue the matter in an adult manner, then you will ask questions. If, however, you believe the criticism should be disregarded, you will defuse and move on.

The simple act of asking a question moves you immediately into a rational, adult position. Genuine inquiry is active rather than reactive. The calm pursuit of information allows you to initiate and guide a dialogue with your critic. It discourages the critic from taking over the conversation. Neither do you take over. Instead, genuine inquiry encourages balanced give-and-take discussion.

Along with putting you in the adult position, genuine inquiry accomplishes several other things:

1. *It forces your critic to think about the criticism.* If the criticism is unwarranted or a generalization, your critic will have difficulty backing it up with concrete facts.

Criticism: "Your staff are a bunch of lazy bums."
Response: "Can you tell me who precisely you think is lazy?"

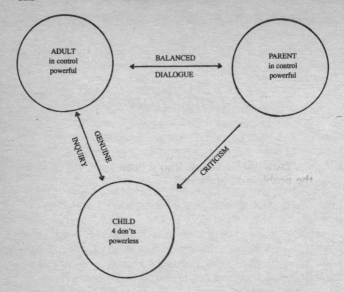

"Well, I don't know. They just seem lazy to me."

"Precisely who is lazy, and what do you mean by lazy?"

"They just don't do anything."

"Are you telling me they don't do their jobs, that they don't send the material out as you need it?"

"Yeah, that's right. They're not sending the material out."

"Could you be more explicit? What material did you not receive on time and who was responsible for it?"

"Well, I don't remember."

"When you have the details, please tell me about it."

If the criticism was well-founded but vague, your critic will be encouraged to give you the specifics you need to use the criticism constructively.

Criticism: "None of your guys gets the stat reports to our division on time."

Response: "Who exactly do you mean by none of my guys? Can you tell me who's been late with his reports?"

"Let me think. Zach handed me his report three days late this week. Come to think of it, his report was late two weeks ago, too."

"Then it's usually Zach who's late?"

"That's right."

"Now that I know who's been late, I'll deal with the problem right away."

Through genuine inquiry this manager was able to pinpoint the problem and do something about it.

2. *Genuine inquiry gives you time to think.* The moment you take to formulate a question and listen to the response gives you time to shake off the flustered feeling criticism often brings. It allows you to bring your feelings back into balance, so that you are prepared to think during the rest of the transaction.

3. *Genuine inquiry puts the ball back in your critic's court.* There is an element of surprise involved here, which you will often see reflected on your critic's face. Give him or her time to recoup. Do not press for an immediate answer to your question. You are not mounting a counterattack; you are genuinely trying to get more information. When you question your critic, never raise your voice or display aggressive mannerisms. Proceed calmly and rationally, pressing your critic gently for concrete information.

4. *Genuine inquiry clarifies things for you.* The criticisms that hook us are usually generalizations, judgments, exaggerations, or personal attacks. By asking questions, you are asking your critic to explain what it is that you *do* that has caused him to label you.

Do not settle for his repeated judgments or attacks. Behavior is concrete. You either do it or you don't.

Question until you know exactly what you do and how often you do it. You will also want to ask for specific examples of your behavior. Once you have this information you can think, sort, and then either agree or disagree with the description of your behavior.

You may agree that in fact you did behave in a certain way, yet disagree that the behavior entitles the critic to judge or label you. For instance, you may have on a given occasion forgotten to do something you had promised to do (behavior). This does not mean you are irresponsible (judgment, labelling).

Questioning forces thought. Responding to questions forces thought. Genuine inquiry helps both you and your critic move from a feeling state to a thinking state. The more you think, the less victimized you will be; the more your critic thinks, the more rational he or she will become. Your goal is to bring as much thinking as possible into the critical dialogue:

Criticism: "You really are disorganized."
Response: "Tell me what I do that makes you say I'm disorganized."
   "You forgot to pick up the dry cleaning yesterday."
   "Yes, I did forget. I do not agree that that makes me disorganized."

By encouraging your critic to think, you may benefit from a poorly expressed but well-intended criticism:

Criticism: "Your presentations at meetings are no good."
Response: "How so?"
   "Well, they don't have an orderly progression."
   "I'm not sure I know what you mean by an orderly progression. Could you be more explicit?"
   "I think you should put an outline on the board and number your topics so that we can follow along as you move from point to point."

"That's a pretty good idea. What else is wrong with my presentations?"

"Nothing, I guess. But I think you would do well to write an agenda on the board."

"I'm going to try that. Thanks."

5. *Genuine inquiry neutralizes negative intent.* If a critic is insensitive, abrasive, or rude—either publicly or privately—genuine inquiry can cool down the situation in a matter of minutes. Genuine inquiry is especially helpful in exposing lies and exaggerations.

Because I happen to be tall and blonde I often hear comments like, "You sure do a lot of work for Fortune 500 companies. It must help to be pretty."

"Do you really think that companies hire me for my looks?"

"Well, it can't hurt."

"How many times do you think I'd be called back if I didn't have something of substance to offer?"

By that time, my critic usually backs down. There is undoubtedly some reason behind a rude comment —insecurity, an unresolved personal problem, a rough day—but that does not mean that I, or anyone else, should bear the brunt of someone else's discomfort.

Having a few questions ready for situations like these can help you deal with such attacks quickly and effectively. My personal favorites are: "What exactly do you mean by that?" and "Why did you say that?" You will want to formulate some of your own.

6. *Genuine inquiry encourages your critic to think before criticizing you in the future.* If you continue to press for specific information, it will be harder for your critic to attack you with generalizations or exaggerations. By exposing your critic, you make it more difficult for him or her to hook you the next time.

Barry criticized his wife, Eve, in public for being uninterested in physical exercise. Eve was less enthusiastic than Barry about working up a sweat, but she participated in many day-long group bike rides, as the people they were with knew.

Barry: "We all know you're a bump on the log, Eve. You sit home while I'm out getting good clean exercise with our friends."

Eve: "Tell me when was the last time I stayed home when there was a group bike ride?"

"Just the other day I wanted you to go on a nice long ride and you wouldn't go."

Eve had declined Barry's invitation; Barry pushed the pace too fast for her. Eve persisted with her original question. "When has there been a group ride that I did not go on?"

"Well, um, er," Barry stammered, "I can't remember."

A few well-put questions will expose any exaggeration, generalization, or lie to everyone in hearing range. Your critic will almost certainly try to circumvent you, so be sure to stick with getting an answer to your original question.

7. *Genuine inquiry is the most effective way to respond to criticisms that are masked as questions.* If you answer a critical question, you will immediately find yourself in a childish defensive position.

Criticism: "You're late! Where have you been?"
Response: "I got a late start and traffic was terrible."
    "A likely story!"

Criticism: "Where did you learn your manners, young man?"
Response: "Well, my parents."
    "I don't know if they knew what they were doing."

Criticism: "Why did you buy that?"
Response: "I like it. The colors are terrific."
    "I think the colors are terrible."

Now let's take these same criticisms and see how you can maintain an adult position by answering with a question of your own.

Criticism: "You're late! Where have you been?"
Response: "How late am I?"
    "Five or ten minutes."
    "I guess I am."

Criticism: "Where did you learn your manners, young
    man?"
Response: "Did I do something to offend you?"
    "Yes, you interrupted."
    "I didn't realize I did that. I'm sorry."

Criticism: "Why did you buy that?"
Response: "Why do you think I bought it?"
    "I guess you like it."
    "Yes, I do like it."

You may not always want to respond to a critical
question with a question; in some circumstances the
result can be damaging. For example, a senior vice
president called one of his vice presidents on the car-
pet. "Why the hell haven't you started using our expensive new computer system? You're slower than
death."

If the junior officer had made a genuine
inquiry—"Exactly what do you mean, I'm slower
than death?"—the senior man might well have taken
that response as fighting words. So his vice president
simply gave the information: "The technicians and
programmers haven't finished the installation yet."

"Oh, I see," the senior vice president said. A calm,
factual answer to a critical question can avert a blow-
up at times when a responding question might be seen
as insubordinate or provocative.

8. *Genuine inquiry stimulates openness and intimacy
when criticism has positive intent.* There will always
be areas of discontent in an intimate relationship. Although you may decide not to change a questioned
behavior, it is important to listen carefully to what
your critic has to say and try to understand his or her

point of view. When you ask questions, you demonstrate a sincere interest in wanting to know the other person.

It is not easy to listen when our intimates tell us we have fallen short in their estimation. If we respond with counterattacks, defensiveness, or interruptions, we discourage the honesty and open communication that are vital to an intimate relationship. We will never really know our intimates and what they think if we do not respond to their suggestions and feedback. Even though facing up to our shortcomings is unpleasant, we cannot deepen our relationships unless we are willing to put aside our learned responses to criticism, and to think and probe for understanding. Also, close relationships provide an excellent opportunity for us to learn more about ourselves. Viewing these exchanges as opportunities to learn and grow encourages our openness.

In an attempt to gain the control over life she was deprived of as a child, Sue, the adult child of an alcoholic, is frequently controlling and critical of others. Her husband, Guy, loves her and recognizes, as she does, the source of her problem. But this does not mean he wants to let Sue run his or their son Jerry's life. To improve their relationship and to help her, Guy was critical of her controlling behavior.

"You had every minute of the weekend planned last week, Sue. Tennis after breakfast, then home to do the laundry. Lunch and a bike ride in the park in the afternoon. Dinner with the Sullivans. Then all day Sunday with your brother and his family. You had Jerry's weekend planned from start to finish, too. I think it would be better if you could back off and give us a chance to contribute and make plans for ourselves."

Because she had been trying to be less controlling, Sue was distressed to hear Guy's criticism, but she used genuine inquiry to keep her feelings from taking over. "I wasn't aware I had taken over last weekend.

Have you noticed any other times when I've done it recently?"

"Yes, I have. When your quilting group was here on Monday night, I heard you telling Wilma which pattern she 'had' to pick for her new quilt."

"Yes, I remember that now. I really appreciate your feedback. Sometimes I just don't realize I'm being so bossy."

"I know that. I also know you're trying hard to change and that you've had a lot of successes."

Working with her husband to solve her problem helped Sue, and her relationship with Guy, to grow.

There are, as we've seen, advantages to using genuine inquiry. There are also some points to remember when employing this technique:

✓ *DON'T:*
1. *Use genuine inquiry as a counterattack.*
2. *Use genuine inquiry until you are ready to enter into an honest give-and-take transaction with your critic.*
3. *Be discouraged if your body responds with the physiological symptoms of danger: red face, rapid breathing, increased heart rate.* No matter how accomplished you become at genuine inquiry and other coping skills, criticism can still pose a threat or be unsettling. Your physiological responses will become less acute as you practice the techniques.
4. *Worry about making a mistake.* You can correct it the next time.

✓ *DO:*
1. *Prepare yourself.* As you did with defusing, take the time to listen to and examine your critic and to plan your responses before speaking.
2. *Ask your questions in a steady, strong voice.* Never overpower your critic with either your tone or your body language.
3. *Establish and maintain eye contact.* This helps you

stay in the adult position and equalizes the balance of
power. Also, your critic will find it harder to circumvent you or squirm away.

If you have had trouble maintaining eye contact in
the past, focus initially on your critic's shoulders,
chin, nose, or cheeks. As you become more comfortable, move on to direct eye contact. Use affirmations
to enhance your ability: "Eye contact helps me establish an adult position. It feels fine. I'm getting more
comfortable with it every day."

4. *Ask questions about behavior.* Press gently for specific, concrete facts about what you are doing. Don't
let your critic answer your questions with repeated
generalizations, exaggerations, or personal attacks.
You may have to ask three, four, or five clarifying
questions to get the information you need. Keep asking until you are satisfied that you understand the situation.

5. *Take time to think about your response.* You do not
have to respond to a criticism until you have thought
about it carefully and are ready to make a rational
response. This can take half a second or half a week.
If you need time to respond, tell your critic you want
to think about the comment. Then say when you will
respond.

AN EXERCISE IN GENUINE INQUIRY

The preparation for using genuine inquiry is much the
same as the preparation for defusing. Now that you have
been practicing defusing, you should have the sense of
being much more in control of your behavior. Once you
have attained a degree of comfort with defusing, you will
be ready to move on to this more interactive skill.

✓   *STEP 1*
Read your list of critics again and note those with
whom you would like to use genuine inquiry.

✓ *STEP 2*

Write out your genuine inquiry questions and the dialogue they could lead to with each of your critics.

✓ *STEP 3*

Relax and visualize a successful genuine inquiry dialogue with each of your critics. Imagine exactly what will happen in each one. Really hear your critic's responses; see his or her expression.

✓ *STEP 4*

Write your affirmations. Affirmations will reinforce the power of your imagined dialogues. Here are some examples:

"I really enjoy using this technique. It helps me learn how to use criticism."

"Asking questions puts me immediately in an adult position. I feel a great deal of self-control."

"When I am criticized, I like to be able to interact with my critic on an adult level. This skill really works."

"I am ready to use genuine inquiry with——. I know how to do it now. I feel good about the outcome."

"Genuine inquiry produces an adult-to-adult transaction. It is not used to attack. I look forward to using genuine inquiry and criticism to grow."

✓ *STEP 5*

Do it! Draw on your imagined dialogues to engage in successful genuine inquiry with your critics.

As with defusing, one of two things will happen when you use genuine inquiry for the first time. You meet with success, even if you were a bit hesitant at first. You deliver your questions firmly but calmly; your critic responds; you engage in an adult dialogue. Be sure to congratulate yourself on this excellent outcome.

Or you struggle a great deal and are unable to follow through using genuine inquiry. If this is the case, ask yourself the following questions to examine what caused your difficulty: Was I adequately prepared? Did I envision myself using the technique, hear myself delivering my questions? Was I prepared for my critic's responses? Did I listen carefully to the criticism so that I could ask appropriate questions? Did I let my feelings take over during the transaction so that I was unable to think?

Once you have answered these questions and any others that you might want to ask yourself about the encounter, you undoubtedly will have learned something.

In the southern hospital where I was giving a workshop, I used genuine inquiry to invite an adult-to-adult dialogue with my critics. When I was in a hurry and unable to ask questions, I defused criticism, but when I could devote my time and attention to my critic, I moved on to genuine inquiry.

I was sitting beside a doctor in the cafeteria. He opened a conversation by saying something like, "So you're here to teach our nurses how to be aggressive?"

"Are you concerned about the content of my workshop, doctor?" I asked.

"I sure am. Our nurses are aggressive enough. Why, just the other day one of them turned on her heel and stormed out of my patient's room. I call that impolite and aggressive. What our nurses need is to be more responsive to doctors and patients."

"It sounds as though that nurse must have been pretty angry."

"Well, I guess she was," the doctor agreed.

"Do you have any idea what the content of my course is?"

By this time the doctor had stopped attacking and said, "Well, no, not really."

I explained that I was training nurses to be more direct and assertive so that built-up anger did not result in the type of situation he had just described. "Unfortunately, if nurses feel frustrated and so powerless that they cannot express their concerns or feelings, eventually they explode. This kind of delayed, exaggerated response is embarrassing to everyone—nurses, doctors, and patients, too."

The doctor had listened carefully to what I had to say. "That makes sense."

"I'm training nurse educators in ways that encourage their nursing students to be polite yet direct and straightforward. Assertive behavior is the alternative to passive/aggressive behavior."

The doctor and I then had a lively discussion of the differences between assertive, aggressive, and passive behavior. We spoke about the powerlessness many nurses experience, and we both gained knowledge and insight from the exchange.

A conversation that started with a cutting criticism ended up as an experience of enhanced learning and understanding. Genuine inquiry can be a powerful means of initiating meaningful adult communication.

CASE HISTORIES

Now that the protagonists of these case histories have learned to defuse successfully, they have gone on to use genuine inquiry to open up communication with their critics.

✓ DOMINATE / CONTROL

Anna experienced a great improvement in her self-esteem when she learned to defuse George successfully. As Anna's self-confidence grew, George talked down to her less and less. He became less directive and began to respect her more. On the exercise issue, however, he continued to try to get his way. Anna prepared herself and was ready to use genuine inquiry the next time the issue surfaced.

"Anna, I don't know why you continue to insist on a loosely structured exercise program with friends when you can be part of an ongoing class that will ensure your participation."

"George, don't you know that I'm exercising with my friends on a regular basis?"

"You may have mentioned it. I forget," George hedged.

Anna remained firm and did not defend herself by reminding George of all the times she had mentioned her exercise activities. "I am, and I enjoy it and prefer it to going to an aerobics class."

"Well, do what you want."

"I will."

Genuine inquiry allowed Anna and George to have discussions, whereas before George would have told Anna what he wanted her to do and Anna would have done it. Anna used genuine inquiry to learn why George wanted her to do things his way. Sometimes she would agree with his reasons, sometimes not. In any case, a degree of openness and intimacy that had not previously existed was introduced into Anna and George's marriage.

✓   *MANIPULATION*

Continuing her manipulations, Jenny again brought up the subject of her friend's son Bruce. Through courteous, non-belligerent questioning, Tom was able to show his mother how his and Bruce's situations were different.

"Bruce spends a lot of time with his mother. He really loves her."

"What do you mean by that, Mother?"

Jenny was taken back a bit by Tom's question. He had never reacted that way to one of her digs about Bruce before. "Well, it seems that if a son really loves his mother, he makes an effort to visit her."

"I agree with that. Are you suggesting that because Bruce spends more time with his mother than I spend with you, he loves his mother and I don't love you?"

"Well, not exactly."

"Do you realize that I live three hundred miles away from you and Bruce lives in the same town as his mother?"

"Yes, that's true."

"Don't you think that's a factor in how often I'm able to see you?"

By this time Jenny had had enough. She hadn't gotten Tom to feel guilty with her comment. "We needn't get into this discussion, Tom. I was just making a comment."

Through genuine inquiry, Tom was able to stop being defensive with Jenny. He could make his points about why he was unable to spend so much time with her without the build-up of resentment that so frequently undermines a healthy, loving relationship between adult children and their parents. Genuine inquiry allowed Tom to cope with Jenny's manipulations, a far better response than avoiding her altogether.

✓   *PUNISH / GET EVEN*

After Bill learned that he could defuse Mary's criticisms about his long working hours on the spot, he was ready to try genuine inquiry in order to discourage her from criticizing him on this issue.

In front of a couple they know well Mary remarked, "Bill is never home."

"Never?" Bill said.

"Well, of course you're home. Now and then."

"Do you think you could be making it sound worse than it is, Mary?"

"Well . . ."

One of their friends said, "We're going to get tickets for a concert next month. Would you like to join us?"

"We'll have to see if Bill will stop working long enough," Mary replied sarcastically.

"Mary, do you really think I would refuse an opportunity to go to a concert?"

"Well, I guess not."

Mary may never be satisfied with Bill's choice of long

working hours. But with enough patient, persistent questioning from Bill, she may stop criticizing his decision.

✓ *ABUSE*

An emotionally abusive relationship can easily turn into a physically abusive one if the abusive partner is pushed too hard. An abusive person may take genuine inquiry as an attack—even when the questions are asked calmly and rationally—and may become physically violent. If you are in an abusive relationship, you will want to think carefully about your partner's limits before using genuine inquiry. If you are sure your partner will not become physically violent, genuine inquiry can often get an abusive person to back off. This may or may not discourage further abuse, but it will give you a much-needed boost in self-esteem and increase your personal power.

Margaret did not realize that she had used genuine inquiry before she started working with the support group. She had not questioned Bob directly, but with a mind towards testing the validity of Bob's criticism, she had questioned other people who knew him. She had also questioned herself, recognizing that she might have an unrealistic view of herself. The feedback Margaret got from others and herself convinced her that Bob's attacks were caused not by her behavior but by Bob's own insecurities and over-developed sense of entitlement.

Asking questions, as Margaret did, is a good course for anyone to follow when the same criticism arises consistently from one source or from more than one source. By consulting others you can get some sense of the magnitude of the problem, which will help you to resolve it. Self-scrutiny will supplement the feedback you get from others.

Reasonably certain that Bob would not resort to physical abuse, Margaret began to question him in order to understand why he said the things he did. Bob was adept at getting around her. He denied saying things she was sure he had said; or he told her not to pay any attention to him when he was in a foul mood. But he rarely owned up to his behavior or entered into a rational discussion with her. Bob thwarted many of Margaret's attempts to use genuine inquiry with him, but she did find that she could use it to expose some of his inaccuracies.

"You have a big mouth, Margaret."

"Because I take a stand and disagree with you, you call that a big mouth?"

"Yeah."

"What would you have me do?"

"Just accept what I say." Bob then looked at her with an insidious smile. But Margaret had made her point.

Margaret also learned to ask questions when Bob criticized her in public. Bob made this remark at a party: "I worked hard all day, came home starved and undernourished and when I went to take a nice, fresh brownie, Margaret wouldn't let me have it. Now do you see what I have to put up with?"

"Bob, do you recall what I told you about that plate of brownies?"

"No," Bob challenged. "Did you tell me something?"

"I told you they were for a bake sale and that someone was coming to pick them up."

"That's a likely story," Bob scoffed.

Margaret was unwilling to be Bob's victim in public, but she realized that genuine inquiry in public not only made Bob uncomfortable but also made their friends uncomfortable. So she frequently defused Bob's public criticisms, cutting them short while maintaining her adult position. Later, in private, she used genuine inquiry to address the earlier public criticism.

At times genuine inquiry actually got Bob to think.

"You really are self-centered, Margaret."

"Exactly what do I do that leads you to that conclusion?"

"Well, you always want things your own way."

"Would you give me some examples, Bob?"

"You want all this help from me around the house."

"Do you really think it's unfair of me to ask you to help out at times?"

"I was never asked in the past."

Margaret did not respond to Bob's implicit judgment that she was inferior to his first wife. "I'm different from your ex-wife," she stated firmly.

"You sure are."

Again, Margaret ignored the slight and stuck to her questioning. "Have you ever thought that she left you so abruptly because she had been dissatisfied for a long time but was never able to tell you?" Notice that Margaret did not counterattack by phrasing as fact her interpretation of the break-up of Bob's previous marriage. She merely asked him if he had considered that line of reasoning.

Despite his thick skin, Margaret's question gave Bob a moment's pause. "You may have a point," he said.

Handling abusive criticism with genuine inquiry requires good judgment as well as patience and persistence. Be sure your thoughts and feelings are well balanced before using genuine inquiry on an abusive critic. Sometimes it may be better to defuse than to try to start a more interactive transaction. But if you pick and choose your opportunities carefully, genuine inquiry will certainly stem the tide of abusive criticism. It may even get the abuser to stop and think.

✔ PROJECT / TRANSFER

Genuine inquiry can expose your critic's attempt to transfer his or her undesirable traits onto you. This, however, does not mean he or she will stop trying. People who project are probably not ready to face their own faults.

Bob often told Margaret she was self-centered.

"What does self-centered mean to you, Bob?" Margaret asked on one occasion.

"You always expect to get your own way and you

don't listen to anyone else's point of view."

"Have you ever thought that you might do that yourself?"

"I don't do that," Bob said indignantly.

Bob may not be ready to admit it yet, but he might think about what Margaret has said.

You cannot make someone ready or able to accept his or her faults, but this does not mean you allow that person to continue projecting. Genuine inquiry is a way of gently leading someone who projects to self-examination.

✓ *SLICE*

Cynthia used questions to keep her colleague, Stan, from inflating his self-esteem by taking chunks out of hers. At times, Stan even talked himself into a corner— proving how nasty and thoughtless his criticism was in the first place—when trying to come up with answers to Cynthia's genuine inquiries.

Stan: "You're too sensitive."

Cynthia: "Are you saying I'm too sensitive because I talk to you about my feelings?"

"Yes, you shouldn't be so sensitive."

"Do you think I'm any more sensitive than anyone else, or am I just more open about my feelings?"

"Well, I sure don't understand how you come up with half the stuff you do."

"I'm sure you don't."

Stan frequently questioned Cynthia's competence, saying things like, "I can't stand it when you make statements you can't back up."

"What makes you think I can't back them up?"

"Well, can you?"

"Yes, I can."

Cynthia was prepared to back up her statements, but she waited until Stan challenged her to do so. Had she responded to his original statement with evidence of her own position, she would have been defending herself. Questioning showed Stan she was not willing to be the victim of his slices.

She was also unwilling to sit by when Stan denigrated women in general.

"A woman could never figure that problem out," Stan said one day about a difficult glitch in a software program their department was writing.

"Why do you say that?" Cynthia asked in a firm but unaggressive way.

"Because it's true."

"I'm a woman, aren't I?"

"Ye-e-s," Stan said cautiously, not sure where Cynthia was going with her question.

"Do you think I can fix this glitch?"

"Well, you're different," Stan said triumphantly.

Cynthia smiled. "I don't know. Last time I looked in the mirror I saw a woman."

Stan ended up looking very foolish indeed. Note that Cynthia did not goad or taunt Stan or try to belittle him. She merely used genuine inquiry to lead him to the logical conclusion of his original statement.

✓   *GET ATTENTION*

Defusing usually works very well on attention-seekers, but if you have a sense that you can expose and discourage the behavior with genuine inquiry, by all means use it.

Jonathan did this in a meeting when Herb challenged his group's ability to accomplish a task in a month's time.

"Do you know exactly what our plans are, Herb?"

"Well, uh, no," Herb admitted.

"Then why don't you listen to the rest of my presentation. If you have any unanswered questions, I'll speak to you after the meeting."

Herb continued to attack. "I know you haven't had time to research this thoroughly."

"Can you tell me where you got that information?"

"It's common knowledge."

Jonathan refused to accept this generalization. "I would like to know exactly where you heard it."

"I'm not going to say," Herb said stubbornly.

"If you're going to interrupt my presentation, I'd appreciate it if you could give me some concrete information."

Jonathan did not counterattack. He did not raise his voice, call Herb names or take an aggressive posture. He simply asked questions and made a reasonable request. Herb's behavior may have looked a bit childish to the others at the meeting, but that's because Herb himself was behaving childishly, not because Jonathan was attacking him.

✓ *CHANGE YOU*

Tony used genuine inquiry with Jane to get more information about why she was trying so hard to change him. His goal in using the technique was to have a meaningful exchange on the topic.

"Your clothes are boring and conservative. It's time you wore something more exciting," Jane said.

"Before we were married, you never said anything about my clothes. Am I dressing differently now?" Tony asked.

"No, but that's not the point. I just didn't bring it up before we were married."

"Does that mean you never liked the clothes I wore?"

"No. You look all right in some of the things you wear. There are just a bunch of things I don't like."

"Can you tell me exactly what you don't like about them?"

"They're just what everyone else wears. You should wear clothes that are more stylish and up-to-date."

"Jane, that just wouldn't be me."

"It could be."

"I wouldn't feel comfortable in those kinds of clothes. I'm not going to change the way I dress now."

In this exchange, Tony did not get Jane to open up much about why she wanted to change him. He did not attain his goal of a give-and-take discussion. But he did stay in the adult position and was able to state firmly that he was not going to change just because she wanted him to. Genuine inquiry may not always foster the openness and intimacy you may desire in a close relationship, but it will empower you and allow you to remain in control of yourself in the face of criticism.

✓   *SHOW YOU WHO'S BOSS*

Genuine inquiry is a good way of not throwing the baby out with the bathwater. Kimberley was annoyed and frustrated by Alex's constant attempts to remind her he was her boss. But she also recognized that Alex had some good ideas. She learned that genuine inquiry allowed her to expose his needless criticisms and take advantage of his helpful ones.

Alex: "I don't like your approach. Do it this way."

Kimberley: "Exactly why should I do it that way instead of the way I proposed?"

"We've always done it that way."

"Don't you think it would be a good idea to try something new for a change? I think we'll get the job done quicker this way."

"Okay, you could be right. We'll give it a try."

In this case, by asking for information, Kimberley exposed Alex's criticism as having no firm basis. Alex saw that she had made her proposal for a good reason.

Another time when Alex made the same comment, Kimberley again asked for specific information about why his way was better.

"We tried to do it your way last year. It seemed like a good idea at first, but in the long run the job took twice as much time."

"Don't you think it might be worth another try?"

"I really don't think so. The work piled up and it took us a couple of months to get back on schedule."

This time, Alex had good reason for criticizing her and Kimberley learned that her method had been tried once unsuccessfully. Through genuine inquiry Kimberley brought a measure of give-and-take to their working relationship.

✓ *GET YOU OFF THE TRACK*

Careful questioning can redirect the focus of a conversation when a critic tries to divert you. Jim used the technique successfully with Steve.

"Steve, you didn't get your status reports in on time the last two weeks."

Steve attempted to divert Jim's attention by criticizing him. "Now that you're manager, you sure are getting uppity."

"Is it uppity to expect you to get your reports in on time?"

"You used to do the same thing when you and I were working side by side."

"Does that make it right, Steve?"

"Why are you singling me out? Plenty of others are late with their reports."

"What makes you think I'm singling you out?"

"Have you chewed them out?"

"What makes you think I haven't?"

Steve may never admit responsibility for getting his reports in on time, but with genuine inquiry his diversionary tactics do not either make Jim relinquish his adult position or prevent him from getting his job done.

✓ *UNDERMINE*

Questioning critics who subtly undermine you or talk about you behind your back is one of the best ways of smoking them out. These critics rarely work out in the open, and their behind-the-scenes attacks can harm not only the individuals at whom they are aimed, but entire organizations as well. Open questioning destroys both the camouflage and the effectiveness of snipers.

Rita found this technique worked very well on Sally's attempts to "get" her. In a meeting when Rita made a suggestion, Sally piped up in an apparently kind voice, "We know this isn't your strong point, Rita."

"What do you mean?" Rita asked.

"Well, I mean that little error you made about three months ago." Sally went on to explain in detail what Rita had done wrong.

Rita kept her feelings under control and showed a great deal of strength when she answered, "I did make a mistake in the past. What I love about mistakes is that they're great teachers."

Rita addressed Sally's back-biting in this way: "Sally, I'm told that you're unhappy about my decision to change some aspects of our marketing approach. Are you?"

Sally is not used to straightforward communication and takes a moment to recover. "Well, um, yes, I am."

"If you have a problem with my decisions, I'd appreciate it if you'd come to me instead of complaining to other people. I can't help you with a problem or address your concerns if you don't come to me directly."

Exposing sabotage is about the only way I know to discourage it. If snipers think they can continue to get away with taking potshots at you, they will. If you take away their camouflage, they can't.

✓ VENT FEELINGS

Using genuine inquiry when your critic is venting emotion is tricky. On the one hand, questions can interrupt the venting process and leave the critic full of unexpressed emotions. On the other, questions can help to move the encounter forward to discussion. With experience you will learn when it is better simply to let your critic blow off steam, and when you can effectively use genuine inquiry to help the venting process and bring about a more rational dialogue. Whichever you decide, remember to keep your own feelings in balance and not take the criticism personally.

Here is an exchange between two sisters, Marge and Kathy, who share an apartment. Marge has been on edge recently because of a stressful situation at work.

Marge: "This place is a mess! I can't find anything around here."
Kathy: "What are you looking for?"
   "How can you let this place get so disorganized?"
   "What are you looking for? Maybe I can help."
   "I can't find my tennis racket."
   "Here it is."

In this case Kathy didn't try to get to the root of her sister's bad temper. She asked questions to solve the immediate problem. By not taking Marge's remarks personally, she kept the outburst from escalating into a full-fledged row.

Louise walks into the living room and finds her husband, Peter, reading the paper. She explodes. "You never do anything around here. All you do is sit and read the paper."

"I never do anything around here?" Peter asks.

"Not that I can see."

"Who spent three hours cleaning the garage yesterday?" Peter is careful not to use a self-righteous tone when asking this quetion.

"Well, that was yesterday." Louise starts to cool down.

"What do you really want?"

"I'm tired. Can you help me clean up the kitchen?"

"Sure."

Peter used genuine inquiry to find out what was bothering Louise. Out of tiredness, she made an unwarranted generalization about him. His questions brought her thinking back into operation. She didn't really believe Peter never helped around the house; she was just tired and wanted help cleaning up the kitchen. She vented her feeling and was able to ask rationally for the help she wanted.

✓   *GET ONE'S OWN WAY*

Genuine inquiry can help irritable short fuses to see how unreasonable their demands are. They may not stop making the demands, but you can at least expose the flaws in their argument without fighting back.

Sarah had to question Larry extensively to get him to see how restrictive his rules for "peace and quiet" were for the others in the household. She was careful not to back down, no matter how loud and irascible Larry got. Eventually, her reasoned, logical approach began to get through to him.

"Sarah, how many times do I have to tell you that I don't want a bunch of kids traipsing through this house all the time? This is not a teen club."

"Are you saying you don't want your children to have their friends in to socialize?"

"I'm not saying that. I just want some peace and quiet."

In the basement playroom, the kids have the stereo at a reasonable level. Occasional shouts and laughter can be heard. "Are they making that much noise?"

Larry can't admit the children are relatively quiet today. "They're making enough noise. I can hear them."

"Aren't there times when we have our friends in and the children have to put up with our noise late at night when they're trying to sleep?"

"What are we supposed to do? Go out all the time? They're kids. They have to like it or lump it," Larry yells.

Sarah ignores the blow-up and focuses on asking questions. "Are you saying they don't have any rights?"

"Sure they have rights," Larry grudgingly allows.

"When we live with other people we pay the price of being inconvenienced at times."

"Well, I don't like it."

"I'm sure you don't. Who said having kids was always going to be easy or convenient?"

The next time the children had their friends over one of them had brought a new record album. The music was pretty loud and not the kind Larry likes. He exploded.

"Boy, Sarah, you sure want everything your own way, don't you?"

Talk about the pot calling the kettle black, Sarah thought to herself to vent her rising anger. She was unwilling to let Larry tag her with an undesirable label, especially when it was one that could be applied to him. She did not, however, match Larry's rudeness with her own and get into a shouting match with him. Instead, she maintained her control and asked calmly, "Exactly what do you mean by that?"

"First you want all these kids in the house, and now you let them play all that crazy music."

"And that means that I want everything my way?"

"I give you an inch and you take a mile."

"Are you telling me that just because the kids and their friends are here listening to their music that you're giving a mile?"

"Didn't you ever hear the saying, 'A man's home is his castle'?"

"Yes I have."

Meeting Larry's criticisms with genuine inquiry kept Sarah in an equal position in the transaction. Little by little she began to lengthen her husband's short fuse.

✔ *GET A LAUGH*

When the joke is on you—or on a group or someone who isn't present—genuine inquiry can expose and discourage the joker. Questioning the joker gives him or her the opportunity to examine the consequences of toxic humor. Whether you question the joker privately or publicly will depend on the situation. If you believe you may initiate a good discussion among a group, then question the joker in public. If you think you will embarrass the joker or members of the group, it would be better to take the joker aside later.

You might respond to an ethnic joke by saying, "What if someone here belonged to that nationality? Would you still tell that joke?" Or to a sexist joke with, "Would you like it if someone told a joke like that about your mother or your wife?" You could also say, "Do you think you could get a laugh without getting it at anyone's expense?" These kinds of questions invite the person to think more deeply about the jokes he or she is telling. Above all, do not laugh at toxic humor. If you do, you play right into the joker's hands and any questions you ask will not be taken seriously.

When you use genuine inquiry with a joker, remember to press for explicit examples. For instance:

A female executive at a meeting: "You men sure are rotten listeners. You need to take a few lessons from us women."

Response: "What has happened that leads you to believe that one of us is a bad listener?"

Remark made behind Benny's back: "Did you get a load of Benny's tie? He must have picked it up at the circus."

Response: "Why do you object to Benny's tie?"

"Well, it's loud, that's for sure."

"Why do you have a problem with Benny wearing a loud tie?"

"Oh, forget it. I was just kidding."

You may be accused in these situations of not having a sense of humor. That's not, of course, necessarily true. What you surely don't have is a sense of *toxic* humor. Don't let other people's thoughtlessness keep you from trying to discourage toxic humor and prevent the harm it can do.

WHEN INTENT IS POSITIVE

The practice of asking questions is an excellent way to stop ourselves from responding to constructive criticism with the Four Don'ts. The moment we ask a question, we get ourselves out of the child mode and into the adult mode. From this position we can react openly to well-intended criticism and get the most out of it.

All too often we don't switch to an adult position until sometime after the criticism has been delivered and we've had a chance to calm down. In the time lapse, however, we may have lost whatever immediate benefit we might have gained from questioning on the spot. Asking a question when the criticism is made also helps get feelings into balance right away and initiates a dialogue that could be very illuminating.

For example, Warren, an experienced manager, notices that David's division is lagging behind.

"Your group isn't working up to speed, David. I'd like you to get them moving faster."

Immediately, David defends himself. "We're not too far behind considering one of our guys has been out. We're doing our best to keep up."

"Well, you've got to figure something out. If you continue to fall behind, you could slow up the whole division."

"As I said, Warren, it's tough being short-staffed."

"Look, your job is to keep your group up to the production quotas. Fix it."

By defending himself, David set the tone for this parent/child, just-shut-up-and-do-it transaction. Let's take a look at what genuine inquiry could have accomplished.

"Your people aren't working up to speed, David. I'd like you to get them moving faster."

"Which part of the division seems to be lagging, Warren?"

"Group A. They're not keeping up."

"I was afraid that could be a problem. One of my key

people has been out. Do you think I could move someone else in to fill his place?"

"We've gotten into trouble doing that in the past. It's
just robbing Peter to pay Paul."

"I could try to get more time out of my people. But
they're already putting in a lot of overtime as it is."

"Well, give that a try. In the meantime, we can both
be thinking of other alternatives. We'll talk again on
Thursday."

Genuine inquiry not only kept David functioning on
an adult level, it also created a balanced atmosphere for
problem-solving. The very fact that David appeared
open to suggestions encouraged Warren to enter into a
discussion. When David closed himself off by defensiveness, Warren had little incentive to spend his valuable
time helping David solve the problem. But when David
invited Warren's help by asking him for more specific
information, he got the benefit of Warren's cooperation
and experience.

There are many people in your personal and professional life who want to help you with their criticism.
Think about who they are, and prepare yourself to use
genuine inquiry the next time they approach you with
some feedback. Questioning will predispose you to listen
and think about the criticism and put you in a sound
position either to agree or disagree with it. Of course,
even well-intentioned criticism can be wide of the mark.
In that case, express your gratitude for your critic's interest, even though you choose not to act on the feedback that was offered.

Genuine inquiry places us in the adult position and
opens lines of communication. In the latter respect it is
different from defusing, which cuts off communication.
We use genuine inquiry to initiate an exchange of information that will teach us and deepen our understanding
of an issue. Your critic may learn from it, too. Unlike
defusing, genuine inquiry works well with negative or

positive intent. It exposes and neutralizes negative intent; it allows us to take full advantage of well-intended criticism.

Genuine inquiry also lays the foundation for stating a position, the final skill we will discuss.

7

Stating Your Position

OUR OPINIONS ARE not fact, but they are based on fact. Therefore, it is important to do a thorough job of gathering information before forming an opinion about what your critic has said. The skills of silent observation, careful listening, and genuine inquiry are vital for this fact-finding. They will help you gather the information you need to form an opinion. Once you have formed an opinion, you are then ready to agree or disagree with someone else's view.

Forming an opinion does not mean that you are "right" and the other person is "wrong." An opinion is not right or wrong. Furthermore, opinions can change, and often do as we gather more information and think about an issue.

When we confuse having an opinion with being right or wrong, we close ourselves off to new information, further thought, and deeper understanding. We miss many opportunities to learn and grow.

The ability to state your opinion and agree or disagree with your critic depends on your having already completed several preliminary steps. You must have observed and listened to your critic, objectified and detached yourself emotionally, and engaged in genuine inquiry. This final step in the process accomplishes many things:

1. *Stating a position forces your critic to think further about the criticism.* When you have arrived at the point where you can calmly state a position that is different from your critic's, your critic cannot help but notice and respond to your conscientious and thorough efforts. Your preparation puts you in the adult position. This encourages your critic to take you—and your strongly stated position—seriously.

For example, a critic comes to you and says, "Your staff are a bunch of lazy bums."

"Tell me, who on my staff is lazy?" you respond.

"Zach is lazy. Zach does not get his reports in on time."

You have questioned and received a concrete answer from the critic. You now use your skills in observation and genuine inquiry to study Zach's work habits. You question Zach and other staff members. Once you have gathered as much information as possible you come to a conclusion: Zach works hard, but he has put a low priority on getting his reports in on time.

Now you return to your critic. "I've looked into the matter and I agree with you that Zach has handed in his reports late at times. I do not agree with you that he is lazy. He works very hard, but he has placed a low priority on getting reports to you on time."

"I wish he'd put us higher on his list," your critic says. "We need those reports."

"I'll be sure to talk to him about that, or I may give the job to someone else. Zach is already overburdened."

"Fine. Just as long as I get them."

"Now, who else on my staff is lazy."

"Nobody, really. I was just angry about those reports."

"I understand. I'll see to it that you get them on time."

By moving on from genuine inquiry you bring closure to an issue. The problem with the reports has been investigated and resolved. The next time your critic is dissatisfied, instead of making a sweeping generalization, he or she may think first and approach you with a calm, logical presentation of the problem at hand.

2. *When you state a position you establish yourself.* You go on record. You take a stand. This is adult behavior. There is strength in stating a position openly and honestly. Stating your position and agreeing or disagreeing with your critic does not, however, mean that the discussion is over. Your critic could make a counterstatement or ask more questions. During a further discussion you may well learn something that causes you to change your opinion.

Changing your mind still leaves you in the adult mode—assuming, that is, that you do not become defensive or quarrelsome as the discussion continues and deepens. You do not have to quarrel when you state a position. You do not state your position as fact; you state it as your opinion. This is not aggression, it is self-assertiveness. It is a way of building your personal power.

3. *Stating a position helps you clarify your own values.* The process of gathering information and thinking about it naturally leads you to set priorities and understand your own values better. Once you have a clear-cut picture of your priorities and values, day-to-day decisions become much easier to make.

For instance, when I was divorced my children were three, four, and five years old. I faced criticism regarding the children's emotional and financial well-being as a result of the divorce. I listened carefully to the criticisms, paid attention to the intent of my critics, and asked a lot of questions. As I sorted through all this information, I noticed what I was taking to heart and what I was setting aside. Then I asked myself why I was listening to one aspect of a criticism and not another. I came to the conclusion that this process had forced me to think about my priorities and values. I knew now what I wanted to do and why. Therefore, certain criticisms and advice, even though well intended, did not suit my objectives.

I had learned that there were three important things I wanted: a happy home, enough money to live comfortably, and the freedom to be on hand most of the time to bring up my three young children. Once I knew what was important to me, the rest came more easily. I decided to work only part time, even though that meant turning down a number of job opportunities. When others criticized me, I was able to state my position clearly and strongly. This enhanced my sense of personal power and enabled me to stick to the decisions I had made in the face of some rather strong criticism.

For example, someone close to me said, "You're wasting yourself in that small town. Why don't you move to a bigger city where you can get a high-powered job?"

"I've given that a lot of thought," I said. "And I don't think I'm wasting myself. Right now, I think it's more important for me to be able to spend a lot of time with the kids. I also believe they should be close to their father. I am doing what I want to do. I wouldn't feel comfortable with myself if I moved the children away from their father and worked full time. They're too young."

I believed this criticism was well intended, but knowing my priorities and values helped me state my position and disagree with my critic. We had a lot of discussions on this topic, and my friend frequently made excellent points, but I knew what I wanted and what was right for me at the time. We agreed to disagree.

4. *Stating a position is open and honest, and nothing nurtures meaningful communication more than open-*

ness and honesty. When you can state and maintain a position without needing or trying to get your critic to agree with you, because you are not behaving in a threatening or belittling way, your critic has the freedom to return your openness and honesty.

5: *Stating a position exposes and neutralizes negative intent.* Genuine inquiry does this too, but when you state a position, you go one step further. When your position is clear and based on a sound fact-gathering process, it is hard for a critic to generalize, exaggerate, or lie.

Lisa is a junior associate in her father's law firm. She is young but has excellent courtroom presence. Her father and the other partners have noticed Lisa's talent in this area and believe she has the potential to become a top-notch defense lawyer. To give her the experience she needs, they assign her many courtroom cases.

Scott, an associate with more seniority, feels slighted because he is not assigned the type of cases Lisa gets. He has made frequent cutting remarks to Lisa. Lisa has asked her father and the other partners why Scott is not given more courtroom work. The senior partners agree that Scott's value to the firm lies in his ability to negotiate contracts, not in his ability in the courtroom.

Scott: "It sure must be nice being on the inside track in this firm, Lisa. You get the best cases."

Lisa: "Do you really think I get my assignments because I'm family?"

"I sure do."

"Are you aware of my courtroom record?"

"It's good enough, but that's only because you're Daddy's girl and he gives you the cases you need to get experience. Anyone could do the same if they had half a chance."

"Tell me, what happened at your last three courtroom appearances?"

"Okay, so they didn't go so well. But as I said, it takes time to get experience."

"I don't believe that's the only factor. Different people have different natural talents. I happen to do well in the courtroom; your strength seems to be in contracts."

"Yeah, I can write a good contract, but I still think you get the fun cases because you're family."

"I disagree, Scott. I get them because I do them well."

Lisa was not swaggering or boasting in this exchange. Her record clearly backs her up, as do her conversations with the firm's senior partners. She did not challenge Scott or put him down. She merely used the facts at her disposal to state and support her position. Scott did not change his opinion; he still thinks Lisa is getting special treatment because she's the daughter of a senior partner. But he knows that he cannot taunt or goad her into a fight with his critical statements. His negative intent—to slice—was exposed and neutralized.

6. *Stating a position sets your limits and discourages future criticism.* When you state your position clearly and strongly and set limits, your critic knows exactly what those limits are on a certain issue. He or she does not have to guess what you mean; you have said it. Knowing your limits, your critic may think twice before criticizing you again on that issue.

Barry is the husband who criticized his wife, Eve, in public for what he regarded as her lack of interest in physical exercise. Eve exposed his criticism as an exaggeration in front of the group, but Barry continued to make similar comments. One evening when they got home, Eve said, "I don't like it when you criticize me in public, Barry. Especially when your criticisms are exaggerated."

"Oh, come on, I don't exaggerate."

"You do. What you said tonight was just not true."

"You're too sensitive, Eve. You can't even take a little good-natured ribbing."

"I don't think that your comments are good natured. I think you're trying to put me down."

"I'm not, I was just trying to have a little fun."

"Even so, I don't like it. Not at my expense—or anyone else's for that matter. I want you to stop."

Eve stated her position, disagreed with Barry's explanation of why he made the comments, and set her limits by asking him to change his behavior. Barry may or may not change his behavior—Eve has no control over that—but there can be no doubt in his mind that his wife does not like his behavior and that she disagrees with his explanation of his motives. How Barry behaves is up to him, but Eve has been open, honest, and adult about the problem.

When stating a position,

✓ *DON'T:*

1. *Lock yourself into a set pattern of response with any of your critics.* Just because a person usually criticizes you to manipulate or to punish or to slice does not mean that he or she will always do that. Sometimes that critic's remarks may be sincere and motivated by a desire to produce growth or improvement. Always keep an open mind when listening to criticism. You never know when intent might be positive.

2. *State a position without thinking.* This can send unclear and conflicting signals to your critic. It is one thing to change your position after you get new information and think further, and quite another to grab the first position that floats by. You are not a drowning person in need of a life preserver. Take your time and think before arriving at and stating a position.

3. *State a position from a feeling of insecurity or childishness.* Again, take your time, observe, objectify, and think before you take a position. A position taken

when you are overwhelmed by emotions will be one of weakness, not of strength.

✓ *DO:*

1. *Prepare yourself.* Be sure you have understood and practiced the exercises before beginning to state a position with your critics.
2. *Take as much time as you need to think before stating your position.*
3. *Establish and maintain good eye contact.*
4. *Ask at least one question before disagreeing with your critic.* If you don't do this, you will sound defensive. In the case of an ongoing issue that you and your critic have discussed before, however, state your position without hesitation or questioning. You might want to preface your statement with, "As you know..." or "As we have discussed before..."
5. *Always state your position with strength but without hostility.* Use simple, unambiguous words and get right to the point. Never weaken your statement with words like "maybe," "perhaps," or "possible." If you have a "maybe" or "perhaps" in your position, you have not thought it out thoroughly.

AN EXERCISE IN STATING YOUR POSITION

Consult the chart of your critics. Write out your statements of agreement or disagreement. Visualize delivering your statements. Choose and use some affirmations. Deliver your statements.

Here are some sample affirmations for stating a position:

"I have observed, gathered information, and thought a great deal before arriving at my position. I feel secure in my position."

"My position is not fact. It is based on my unique perspective. There is no right or wrong."

"I am prepared to state my position. I feel confident."

"Everyone is entitled to his or her own opinion."

"I recognize that my critic may disagree with me, and that is okay."

"No matter what the outcome of this dialogue may be, I will remain in the adult position."

"I am excited about the prospect of stating my position and asserting myself."

"I realize it is important to be open and to treat my critic with dignity."

"I look forward to stating my position. It enhances my self-esteem and sense of personal power."

"We all have a right to state a position."

You will probably have noticed that you are far more prepared to move on to stating a position than you were to start defusing or using genuine inquiry. Because of the work you have done thus far, you are feeling more adult and in control of yourself. Criticism does not make you as anxious as it once did. You now have the means to choose your response to criticism, rather than reacting instinctively with the Four Don'ts. You are more aware and more knowledgable. Given these changes, criticism is now becoming a source of power and growth. It is no longer a liability.

If you do not feel this new strength, you may wish to go back and review the other skills before moving ahead. Everyone learns new behavior—and unlearns old habits —at a different speed. Some people need more reinforcement and practice than others. Be sure to take as much time as you need to feel comfortable with these skills.

A successfully stated position is a strongly stated position. The more objectivity, information, and careful thought you put into formulating your statement the stronger it will be. Your critic need not agree with your position. As long as you remain adult, rational, and in control, you have succeeded. Be sure to congratulate yourself for your achievement.

When you do not achieve your desired outcome, ask

yourself questions and learn as much as possible from your mistakes. Undoubtedly you will have questions of your own to ask yourself; here are a few I have found useful.

What triggered my emotions, cut off my thinking, and kept me from stating my position strongly? Have I built up some internal resistance to facing this critic? Did I argue and counterattack when my critic disagreed, rather than listen and question?

By examining the transaction carefully, you will know how you need to change your behavior to ensure success the next time. Try rewriting the encounter in your imagination, allowing it to come out the way you wanted it to. When you next meet this critic it will be easier to state your position.

People who have begun to state a position may wonder, "If I look at these transactions as learning experiences and the other person does not, then isn't it unfair that I am growing and the other person is stuck in her same old position?"

It is unfortunate, but it is not unfair. The issue here is your growth. You have no control over anyone else's growth.

Stating a position grows out of genuine inquiry. An example is my conversation with the doctor at the southern hospital about my workshop. While I discussed the differences between assertive, aggressive, and passive behavior with him, the issue of respect came up. The doctor was concerned that my workshop would cause nurses to lose respect for doctors and their decisions. This doctor felt that unquestioning respect was absolutely vital for good patient care.

"I agree that respect between doctors and nurses is a must in the hospital; I don't think that my workshop will cause nurses to lose respect for doctors."

We then went on to discuss the difference between respect and accepting doctors as infallible. We disagreed on a number of points here, too, but by the time we'd finished our lunch, my critic and I both knew where we stood. We had both increased our knowledge and understanding. Before I left the hospital, the doctor and I had occasion for another discussion. This time, however, we met from the outset on equal ground. He was no longer a critic, but a person with whom I could have a free-wheeling exchange of views and ideas.

CASE HISTORIES

Let us now see how the people in our case histories stated their positions.

✓ DOMINATE / CONTROL

Anna's success with silent observation, careful listening, and genuine inquiry led her to be able to state and maintain her position. George frequently brought up the old exercise issue, and Anna stood her ground, using the "broken record" technique. This is a technique described by Dr. Manuel J. Smith in *When I Say No I Feel Guilty* (Bantam Books Inc., New York, 1975). Without raising her voice, Anna repeated and repeated her position in a calm, consistent manner.

"Anna, I don't know why you insist on continuing that loosely structured exercise program with your friends when you could be part of a class. Then you'd really participate."

"As I've said before, George, I don't believe that being part of a class will ensure my participation."

"Well, you're just not disciplined enough to continue a routine."

"I don't agree, George."

"You've never been disciplined enough in the past."

"I don't agree."

Whenever George harped on her exercise program, Anna became a broken record and stated her disagreement with all his objections.

Then a new issue arose for Anna and George. George

worked long hours and was frequently away on business. Anna decided that enrolling in adult education classes would be a constructive use of her time. George was not pleased with her decision and criticized her for it.

"I don't see why you have to enroll in evening classes. They're a waste of time."

"Do you really think they're a waste of time, George?"

"Of course they are. They're all nonsense."

"I find them very informative and I intend to continue with my classes."

"Well, go ahead, but I think you're wasting your time."

"I disagree; I'm going to go."

When Anna discussed this encounter with the group, some others raised the possibility that George wanted her to stay home to keep him company. Anna thought there could be some truth in this. She decided to raise the issue with George again. This itself was a measure of Anna's progress. Only two months before, she would not have dared bring up the issue again.

"George, I've been thinking about your objections to my evening classes, and I'm wondering why my going bothers you so much."

"You have better things to do with your time, Anna."

"What better things do you think I have to do with my time?"

"Well, we could go to the movies."

"Are you saying that you would like me to drop the classes so that I could do things with you on the evenings when you are home?"

"That would be nice."

"Yes, it's nice to have evenings together. But these classes are important to me, just as your business trips are important to you."

"I have to go on those trips. You don't have to take the classes."

"I want to take the classes."

"So go ahead, if you don't value our time together."

"Because I take these classes doesn't mean that I don't value our time together. Do you understand that?"

Grudgingly, George answered, "I suppose so."

"You don't sound convinced. What bothers you?"

"Well, I'm just used to having you here when I'm home."

"Things do change, George."

"They certainly are changing a lot around here lately."

"These classes are stimulating to me. I feel I'm growing a lot from taking them."

"Don't let me stand in the way of your stimulation."

"I won't. After all, we still have most of our evenings together when you are home."

Notice how many skills Anna used in this encounter: reflective listening, genuine inquiry, stating a position. Where once she would have acquiesced to avoid George's criticism, she was now able to participate in a meaningful discussion with him. She did not get George to like or encourage her to continue with her classes, but she remained firm about her intention to do so with or without his blessing.

✓ *MANIPULATE*

One of the things that annoyed Tom most about Jenny's attempts to make him feel guilty was that she often called him at the office, when he had the least time to pay attention to her. Jenny claimed he never called her and that's why she found it necessary to call him, and she called him at work because "it's so hard to get you at home." Tom regularly called her one evening during the week and on the weekend if he was not out of town. Finally he learned to disagree and set limits with her.

"I do not want you to call me at work, Mother. I have a waiting room full of patients and I cannot take time from them to speak with you."

"I only call you at work, Tom, because you never call

me. This is the only time I can get you."

"That simply is not true. You can call me at home in the evenings. Besides, I call you once or twice a week. I do not want you to call me at work."

Asking questions and stating his position kept Tom from getting defensive when his mother criticized him for not visiting her enough.

"I don't suppose you'll have time next month to get away and come and visit your mother?"

"What are you trying to say?"

"I must be the last person on your list when it comes to considering the important people in your life."

"I disagree with that, Mother. I think and care about you a great deal. I cannot get away every month to visit you."

"If you really cared you could come and visit more often."

"I don't agree with that at all. I certainly can care and not visit you every month. I can't visit you every month, and I feel bad that you equate that with a lack of caring."

Without feeling guilty, Tom was able to tell Jenny exactly how he felt about her attempts to manipulate him. In time, Jenny got the message that Tom was not going to give in to her demands. Her habit of making manipulative remarks diminished somewhat, but not entirely. The difference was in the way Tom responded to her manipulations. He did not get hooked, so he was not resentful and did not try to avoid Jenny. He was also able to accept his mother's behavior; sometimes he was even amused by her most blatant manipulations. Because Tom was able to remain in the adult position, their relationship improved.

✓ *PUNISH / GET EVEN*

Bill learned to thwart Mary's attempts to punish him in public for his long working hours by stating his position in a clear, calm voice.

"Bill is never home."

"Never?"

"Well, you're home some, but you work awfully long hours. I hardly see you anymore."

"I know, I am working long hours these days. It's tough on both of us."

"It sure is."

By stating his position and staying in the adult position, Bill could take both his and Mary's feelings into account and deal with them in a straightforward manner.

✓   *ABUSE*

Abusive critics may try to circumvent genuine inquiry with lies, memory losses, or changes of subject. Bob tried all these ploys with Margaret, which often made genuine inquiry an unsuccessful technique for her. She found, however, that stating her position forcefully and using the broken record technique worked well for her.

Margaret, used to professional success as an editor for a national magazine, was finding it hard to launch her career as a free-lance writer. Still, she worked hard at her writing and was starting to get a toehold in this difficult field. She felt vulnerable professionally, and Bob knew it. So he frequently aimed his sarcasm and put-downs at Margaret's career.

At a dinner party Bob remarked, "Margaret's one of those would-be writers who can afford to dabble in writing articles and short stories from time to time because she has a husband to support her."

Margaret was speechless. How could Bob publicly ridicule her about something she took so seriously? Especially when she had worked so hard to cope with his criticism and to try to get him to see what his critical remarks were doing to their relationship. She was unable to cope at that moment; all her hard-won skills simply deserted her. On the drive home from the dinner party she was finally able to pull herself together, and by the time they got home she had recouped well enough to confront Bob.

"Bob, I do not like it when you make derogatory comments about my writing in public."

"Oh, Margaret, I was only teasing."

"That is not teasing. I don't like it, and I want you to stop."

"You can't even take a joke. You're so touchy."

"I don't want to be the target of your jokes. Don't try to get a laugh at my expense."

"You take this too seriously."

"I am not going to put up with it, Bob. Cut it out."

"For crying out loud, Margaret, everybody does it. Why are you such a prima donna?"

"Everyone does not do it. I do not agree that my position on public put-downs and ridicule makes me a prima donna. It does make me unwilling to bear the brunt of your sarcasm. Cut it out."

Margaret gave the same answer to each of Bob's comebacks: I don't like what you do; stop doing it. She became a broken record. No matter how hard a critic's head is, eventually the broken-record phrase sinks in. At the least, it cuts off his comebacks.

When circumstances permitted, Margaret stated her position when Bob criticized her in public.

"Margaret has the easiest life," Bob said to a group one night, "and she still complains that I don't help her enough. You women are home all day and you don't do a thing."

"Bob, do you really think I have free time during the day?"

"Sure you do."

"I disagree, Bob. I certainly don't have free time during the day."

Margaret did not stoop to defense by enumerating all the things she does during the day. She simply put herself in the adult position by asking a question and maintained that position by disagreeing with Bob's statement.

Margaret made a point of taking a stand each time Bob resorted to name-calling in public, either at the time of the criticism or later, in private. By taking a stand, she maintained her dignity and discouraged his behavior. His abuses did not stop altogether, but Margaret held on to her self-esteem in the face of derogatory labels.

"You're a bitch, Margaret."

"Why do you continually call me a bitch?"

"It's just a term I use."

"Stop using it."

Eventually, Margaret won reluctant respect from Bob. He was still moody, threw tantrums, and at times escalated his abuse to test her newly recovered assertiveness. But she did not back down, and her situation improved. In time, Bob did change his behavior in response to the limits she repeatedly set. As a result, their relationship was less chaotic and Margaret was no longer a victim.

✓ *PROJECT / TRANSFER*

When Bob tried to project his faults onto Margaret she blocked him by stating her position.

"You're really self-centered, Margaret."

"What do you mean?"

"All you think about is taking care of yourself—first, middle, and last."

"I just don't agree with that, Bob. Not at all."

Bob could maintain his position. But so could Margaret. She simply would no longer accept his cruel projections.

✓ *SLICE*

When someone continually aims slicing criticisms at you, it isn't always necessary to use genuine inquiry before stating a position. You can state it immediately in response to the slice. Cynthia chose to continue to question Stan before stating her position because she still wanted to invite better communication between them.

"You're too sensitive, Cynthia?"

"Are you saying I'm too sensitive because I have

deep feelings and talk about them?"

"Well, yes. You shouldn't be so sensitive."

"Perhaps you think I shouldn't be sensitive, Stan, but I enjoy my capacity to feel things deeply."

Or, "You're stupid, Cynthia."

"Why do you say I'm stupid?"

"You made a mistake in this calculation."

"You're right. I made a mistake, Stan. But I don't think that makes me stupid."

It took a while, but Stan came to see that he could not damage Cynthia's self-esteem and boost his own with his slicing remarks. They become less frequent and less deeply cutting.

✔   *GET ATTENTION*

Jonathan stated his position and set limits to stop Herb's attention-getting efforts without attacking or becoming hostile.

"I don't think your group can accomplish that in only a month, Jonathan. They're not real swift."

"I don't agree with you there, Herb, and if you keep interrupting, we certainly won't be swift. Save your questions till I've finished. If I haven't satisfied you by then, you and I will sort it out."

At another meeting, Herb interrupted Jonathan again. "Don't you remember what happened to Sal when he used that supplier?"

"I had forgotten that incident, Herb. But let's talk about it when I've given an overview of the project. I'll make a note to get back to it."

Despite knowing that Herb interrupted so frequently to get attention, Jonathan kept an open mind. Careful listening told him that this time Herb had a valid point. By tabling Herb's suggestion until a more appropriate time, rather than dealing with it on the spot, Jonathan showed he was not a pushover. And his openness commanded respect from everyone at the meeting.

✓	*CHANGE YOU*

Tony tried to deal with Jane's attempts to change him by setting limits and stating his position. This helped Tony retain his self-esteem while in a difficult marriage, and to hold on to it when the marriage broke up.

"Your clothes are boring and conservative. It's time you wore something more exciting."

"We've talked about this before, Jane. I'm comfortable with the way I dress; I'm not going to change it."

Or, "Why don't you mingle more? You could move up a lot quicker if you were more gregarious."

"We've had this discussion before, Jane. I'm comfortable with my personal style; it has served me well."

"If it had served you so well, you'd have gotten that promotion already."

"I'm comfortable with my style the way it is."

"Well, you won't move ahead as fast as you could."

"I totally disagree. I've moved ahead very quickly in my organization, and I intend to continue doing so in a way that works for me."

"I still think you could be more outgoing."

"I'm sure you do. But I am what I am, and I would like you to stop trying to get me to behave the way you think I ought to. I do not intend to change."

Jane never did see his point of view, but his ability to set limits and state his position stopped Tony from making changes that would have been harmful to his self-esteem.

✓	*SHOW YOU WHO'S BOSS*

Once Kimberley was able to sort out Alex's useful criticisms from the ones meant only to show her he was boss, she was able to set limits and state her position.

Before a big business trip, Alex said to her, "I want a more detailed itinerary from you."

"How so?"

"I want to know what you expect to accomplish with everyone you'll be seeing."

"Did my work on my last trip meet your expectations?"

"Well, yes."

"Do you think I'm wasting my time?"

"No, not exactly."

"I don't think justifying my itinerary is a good use of my time. Since my trips pay off, I believe my time is better spent preparing for them."

Alex backed off from Kimberley's firm stand. He could offer no good reason, other than that he was boss, for his request. Kimberley did not always use this tactic with Alex. At other times, when his criticisms were well intended and well founded, she was able to listen and learn a great deal from him. She could face him openly, even when changing her opinion and accepting his point of view. She felt adult and in control of herself; their working relationship continued to improve.

✔ *GET YOU OFF THE TRACK*

Using the broken record technique to state your position can be useful with someone who continually tries to sidetrack you. Jim did this with Steve:

"Steve, you didn't get your status reports in on time the last two weeks."

"Now that you're manager, you sure are giving me a hard time."

"That's not true. I simply want your status reports in on time."

"Boy, aren't we touchy?"

"It may appear that way to you. I simply want your status reports in on time."

Eventually, Steve may get the point. Jim isn't trying to strong-arm him or single him out. He just wants him to do his job. Steve may never get on the track, but that is no reason for Jim to get sidetracked. Stating his position and setting limits help him meet his own work goals.

✔ *UNDERMINE*

Part of the underminer's strategy can be making faces

or gestures behind your back, especially when other people are around. When this happens, it is important to confront the situation, state your position, and set limits. It is also important to solicit the input of other people present.

For example, a manager noticed one of his staff making faces at a weekly meeting. Through questioning, he learned that this staff member felt these meetings were a waste of time. The manager immediately asked the rest of his staff for their honest opinion of the meetings. The majority felt they were useful and the manager clearly stated his intention to continue them. If, on the other hand, the group had reported that they did not feel the meetings were useful, he would have had to deal with that response openly and honestly.

There is nothing wrong with facing a problem in public and fixing it. By addressing an issue openly, you remain strong and in the adult position.

Rita noticed Sally whispering at a meeting. "I noticed you talking to Doug, Sally. Do you have a question?"

"Oh, no, no questions."

Rita was not prepared to let Sally slither away, as snipers often try to do. She persisted. "I caught a few words that you said and it sounds to me as if you don't agree with my proposal. Let's talk about it."

"You must have misunderstood. It's fine with me."

Even though Sally denied that she disagreed with Rita and Rita accepted her denial, the mere fact that Rita had confronted her brought Sally's behavior out into the open. Sally was no longer about to camouflage her assaults.

Now suppose Sally had said she didn't agree with Rita's proposal. Rita still must pursue the matter.

"Can you tell me what your problem is with the proposal, Sally?"

"Yes. It's not well prepared."

"Can you be specific?"

"Well, I just think you could have included more details."

"What details do you think are missing?"

"You could have given more examples."

"I disagree. I think that would belabor my points and make the proposal too long."

Rita has successfully smoked out Sally's subtle criticisms and disagreed with them. If Sally continues to be disruptive, Rita will need to set limits by saying something like, "Individual conversations during the meeting don't help. Let's all discuss what you have to say."

Underminers will get away with as much as you let them get away with. Stating a position and setting limits is a very useful tactic to use with this type of critic.

✓ *VENT FEELINGS*

It is difficult to state a position and set limits when people are in the middle of venting feelings. After they have calmed down, you may state your agreement or disagreement and set limits concerning their behavior.

Fran took this tack with Martin. Passing her group one day while they were on a coffee break, he said loudly, "What a bunch of lazy bums, all sitting around doing nothing."

After calming down her staff, Fran returned to Martin. "Earlier, you said my staff was lazy. What makes you think so?"

"They were all sitting around drinking coffee."

"It was their break time. Taking their regular break does not make them lazy."

"Every time I see them they're taking a break."

"I don't buy that, Martin. They only take their regular breaks. I would appreciate it if you would stop criticizing my staff when you don't know all the details."

Fran was not about to have her staff unfairly maligned, even if Martin needed to let off some steam. By not standing up for her people, she would have damaged her own working relationship with them. Stating her position and setting her limits helped Fran contain the effects of Martin's vents.

✓ *GET ONE'S OWN WAY*

People with short fuses can be explosive, loud, and intimidating. Stating your position and setting limits consistently and without faltering helps you confront this undesirable behavior and yet stay in the adult position. Taking a stand reminds short fuses that they are not the only people with needs or rights.

Sarah learned to do this when dealing with Larry. She frequently waits until Larry has cooled down before she begins to ask questions or take a stand.

"I've told you a million times, Sarah. I don't want a bunch of crazy kids traipsing through this house and playing that awful music. You're asking too much when it comes to these kids!"

After a few minutes of this, Larry comes up for air and Sarah speaks. "Are you telling me that because the kids are here listening to records that I am asking too much?"

"You bet. I've given in enough. No more kids in the house."

"I don't think you have given in enough. This is the children's home. They should be able to have their friends in it."

"Well, it's too much."

"I don't agree. Let's be fair. They should be able to do things with their friends at home. I don't want them in the streets."

"But they're here all the time."

"All the time?"

"Yes."

"That's not true. Think about it. They spend a great deal of time at outside activities, and they go to other kids' homes, too. I want them to feel comfortable about bringing their friends here. I will not see them turned away."

Sarah was persistent and consistent in her refusal to let Larry have his way on this issue. He never did learn to like rock, but he did become somewhat resigned to

Sarah's determination to see that their children were able to entertain their friends at home.

✓   *GET A LAUGH*

If you are the recipient or an observer of toxic humor and want to put a stop to it, then taking a position and setting limits makes a great deal of sense. People who use toxic humor can be discouraged when they see that you honestly do not like it.

When someone tells an ethnic joke around you, you might say, "I disagree with the inference in this joke that this ethnic group is inferior. Therefore, I don't think these jokes are funny and would appreciate it if you didn't tell them around me."

Here are some examples of how to deal with toxic humor by stating a position:

"You women sure have to keep on your toes to keep up with us."

"We sure do, and we do a pretty good job of it, too."

"Uh-oh. From this report it looks as if we're leading up to another of Howie's crazy ideas."

"Why do you call his ideas crazy?"

"They're weird and unconventional."

"True, Howie's ideas are different. But I don't think they're weird or crazy. His ideas are innovative, exciting, and productive, and I'd hate to see him discouraged. He is a great asset to this group."

Instead of getting an expected laugh from this remark, Howie's critic learned that Howie is a highly valued employee in some quarters, and will probably think twice before taking a cheap shot at him again.

STATING A POSITION WHEN INTENT IS POSITIVE

When someone has taken the time and the risk to criticize you, it is important to listen carefully, ask appropriate questions, and arrive at a conclusion for yourself so that you will be able to use the criticism if you agree with it or disregard it if you disagree. When you agree with a criticism:

1. *Don't be too apologetic.* By all means, acknowledge your errors and show your willingness to improve, but remember that begging forgiveness can put you right back in a childish position. You have listened to, questioned, and thought about the criticism. Now you may agree or disagree without undue apology.

   Begin to be aware of the number of times you apologize unnecessarily. Apologies are often appropriate, but they can be overused, making you seem weak and timid.

   Criticism: "Your reports are late."

   Response: "Yes, sir. I know they're late. I'm terribly sorry. It won't happen again. In fact, next week they'll be three days early, I promise."

   This is overly apologetic and overcompensates for your lapse. Your response could be: "Yes, sir. I know they're late. I'll see to it you get them on time next week."

2. *Don't add unnecessary excuses.* Your critic is not interested in excuses but in results.

   Criticism: "Your reports are late."

   Response: "Yes, I know they're late. But I had another rush job and then I had trouble with some of my research and my secretary was out for two days and . . ."

   You slip into defensiveness when you do this and fall back into a childish position. An adult response is, "Yes, I know they're late. You'll have the reports before lunch, and I will do my best to get them to you on time next week."

   If, however, you are often unable to get reports in on time because of other demands or consistently unavailable information or some other reason, then you would do well to discuss the problem with the person who expects them. But not at that moment, when the reports are still late and you may be feeling pressured. Instead, wait, gather your thoughts and approach a solution to the problem later, perhaps by means of a skill we discuss later called the TACTful message.

3. *Brooding about whatever it is you were criticized for is unnecessary and unproductive.* Get as much as you can out of a constructive criticism and move on.

4. *Do ask your critic for specific suggestions that may help you solve the problem.*
   Criticism: "Your monthly reports are much too long."
   Response: "Yes, they are long. I recognize that. What do you think I can leave out or shorten?"

5. *Even when you agree with a criticism, you may decide not to take action immediately to correct it.* Be up-front with your critic about this—and with yourself. Why don't you want to put effort into changing now? Do you have a reason? Or are you afraid that change will be difficult or uncomfortable? Avoiding change because you are afraid of it will not help you get the most out of constructive criticism.

When you disagree with a well-intended criticism:

1. *Offer an explanation of your position.* Remember that explaining is not defending. To arrive at your position you have already asked questions and thought about the issue. The explanation you offer can help your critic think further about the criticism and possibly see things from your point of view.

   Jake's boss, Perry, criticized him for spending too much time wooing small accounts. "You're wasting your time," Perry said. "You should concentrate your efforts on the large corporate accounts."

   Jake gave his reasons, but he began defensively: "Do you really think so? I think we have to develop the small, growing companies." Even though his reasons were clear and well thought out, he placed himself in a childish position by defending himself instead of simply stating his disagreement before offering his explanation. The difference is subtle, but can you see how much more in control Jake stays with the following response. He is not answering to Perry, merely answering him.

"I don't agree with you, Perry. I think that any time I spend developing new accounts is time well spent. These small medical supply houses are growing fast. We'll grow with them if we get in on the ground floor. I don't think it's a good idea to stay entirely dependent on our large corporate accounts."

"You may have a point. I'll take a closer look at those companies you've been wooing."

A clear statement of disagreement and a logical explanation can go a long way towards making your critic see your point of view.

2. *Demonstrate your appreciation for genuine concern from someone entitled to comment.*

    Criticism: "You're not helping your son enough with his decision about what college to attend. He clearly needs stronger direction and recommendations to help him make up his mind."

    Response: "I appreciate your interest, but I don't think it's a good idea to be too directive just now. I've thought about this a lot and I think it's important for him to arrive at his own decision. Right now all I want to do is bring up certain points for him to consider, and ask lots of questions."

You don't want to discourage other people's help and input just because you happen not to agree with them in a given situation. Showing your appreciation will keep their insights available to you.

3. *Don't be afraid to show uncertainty.* Sometimes there are good points on both sides of an issue, and you can

disagree with one part of what your critic has said and agree with another. It is adult and assertive to encourage further openness by saying, "You have a point there, but on the other hand..." Or, "I'm not sure where I stand on that particular issue. I need to think more about it."

Stating a position dots the i's and crosses the t's when coping with criticism. The other skills we have discussed are useful in themselves and essential in leading up to this final and definitive skill. Taking a stand is the adult, forthright thing to do. It is dignified and decisive. And exciting, too, because the process of arriving at a position—whether you agree or disagree with your critic—fosters openness and a willingness to change and grow.

The final skill is giving tactful criticism. Before considering it, let's see how far we've come. Now you have examined your habitual responses to criticism. You no longer have to defend, deny, counterattack, or withdraw in the face of criticism, because you have replaced those childish habits with new adult responses.

Instead of reacting immediately to criticism, you now bide your time with silent observation and careful listening until your thoughts and feelings are in balance. Then you choose the appropriate response. You *defuse* a criticism with negative intent when you want to nip it in the bud and discourage further critical dialogue. Or you use *genuine inquiry* to shed more light on the criticism and to encourage adult, rational discussion. Finally, you *state your position* and offer closure.

Now that you can calmly state and maintain a position in the face of even harsh criticism, or disagree with yet appreciate a well-intended criticism, I am sure you realize just how much you have gained from your diligent study and practice of these techniques.

PART THREE

When Words Help

The TACTful Message: How to Give Criticism

ACCORDING TO CONFUCIUS, *"Not to enlighten one who can be enlightened is to waste a man; to endeavor to enlighten one who cannot be enlightened is to waste words. The intelligent man wastes neither his man nor his words."*

Most people believe giving criticism is tough. Why is that? Actually, there are a number of reasons why we procrastinate or avoid giving criticism.

1. *We don't like to rock the boat.* We see criticism as an invitation to conflict, and we tend to avoid conflict. So even when there are gnawing problems that negatively affect relationships, job performance, or the ability to grow, we do not address them. We prefer to ignore these problems and hope they'll go away by themselves.
2. *We feel uncomfortable when we give criticism.* Since we feel uncomfortable when we get criticism, we project those feelings of discomfort onto the person we want or need to confront. Our assumption that the other person will react badly keeps us from giving criticism.
3. *Giving criticism takes time.* We think that giving careful, constructive criticism is so time-consuming that we would rather avoid it and take up the slack our-

selves. This problem is prevalent among managers who believe that keeping after employees to do their jobs properly is more time-consuming and difficult than doing it themselves.

4. *We believe that giving criticism does not work.* Because we procrastinate about giving criticism, when we finally do give it our uncomfortable feelings have grown so strong that we have to let off steam. The criticism is given in the heat of the moment, thoughtlessly and badly. The response to a poorly delivered criticism is often negative. Therefore, the experience tells us that giving criticism doesn't work very well.

Giving criticism is easier when we recognize its worth.

1. *Criticism uncovers problems.* It does not create them. It is far better to bring problems out in the open than to let them accumulate and harm a relationship, a job performance, or an individual's effectiveness. Calling attention to problems is the first step in solving them.

2. *Criticism saves time in the long run, especially on the job.* A manager may invest time in observing and talking to his or her staff, but the alternative is allowing problems to go unsolved. Then the manager sacrifices efficiency and is not doing the job properly.

3. *Careful, thoughtful criticism stops the build-up of uncomfortable, unhealthy feelings.* Consistent, ongoing criticism is far better than an accumulation of destructive feelings that eventually will have to be vented.

4. *Criticism encourages learning and growth.* Without feedback and criticism, our efforts in many areas could be less effective and less successful.

THE TACTFUL MESSAGE

Preparing your criticisms according to this model will give you an excellent chance of getting your message across. There are four elements in the tactful message:

Tell	Talk about the other person's behavior
Affect	Describe how the behavior affects you, the relationship, or the organization
Change	Request a change in the behavior
Tradeoff	State the positive consequences of a change in behavior.

✓ *TELL*

Before you can tell the other person what the unwanted behavior is, you must observe both the action and the spoken word carefully. Then describe the specific action and/or statement to the person. Do not describe what the person does not do; stick to what he or she does do. Be sure to address behavior, not attitudes. Behavior is objective; attitude is subjective. Also, include the frequency of the action. Do not use words like "always" and "never" when describing the behavior. If you do, the other person is likely to become defensive

POOR	GOOD
You are constantly leaving priority work to help Grace. That's ridiculous because you're falling behind in your own work.	I've seen you at Grace's desk three times today and twice yesterday.
I find that you have a nonchalant and bored attitude when I talk to you about this Project.	When I talk to you about this Project you stare into space and sometimes yawn.
You never listen to me.	Frequently when we have discussions, such as yesterday and this morning, you interrupt me or look around as I am speaking.

and tell you about the one time he or she did not behave
in the way you have just described. Be sure to remain
calm and non-judgmental. Address only one unwanted
behavior at a time.

✓   *AFFECT*

Let the person you are criticizing know how the behavior affects you, the relationship, or the organization.
Express how you feel about the troublesome behavior,
not what you think about the behavior or the person.
Take responsibility for your own feelings. Do not say.

POOR	GOOD
You make me worry. I feel that you are pampering Grace too much.	I'm concerned because your work seems to be suffering. Your last report was late and incomplete.
You put me off and degrade me because you are ignoring me.	I feel put down and ignored when you won't focus on me. Also, I'm concerned about your interest in this important Project because the department is working as a team. One person's enthusiasm will affect another's.
I feel that you are not interested in anything I have to say. You want your way, period. You're spoiled.	I feel ignored and hurt and I'm afraid this does not lead to an open give-and-take relationship, which is what I am looking for and hope that you are, too.

"That makes me feel . . ." Remember, no one makes you feel anything.

Don't say "I feel that . . ." when you mean "I think that . . ." Just because you use the word "feel" does not mean you are talking about feelings. When you describe your feelings, use words like, for example, hurt, angry, frustrated.

If it is inadvisable to express your own feelings, then refer to the adverse effects on the relationship or organization. Be clear, not dramatic. You are negotiating a change in behavior, not trying to make the other person feel bad.

✓ CHANGE

Tell the other person what you want him or her to do instead of continuing the troublesome behavior. Limit

POOR	GOOD
Stay out of Grace's office. She'll figure out her own work if you leave her alone.	I think you'd do better to stay at your own desk and help Grace once or twice a day at most. What do you think?
Stop ignoring me! Hold still and pay attention. This is important.	I would like you to establish eye contact with me so that I know you are listening. If this Project doesn't interest you, let's talk about that.
I want you to pay attention to me for a change!	Please make eye contact when I am talking, and wait until I finish my thought before you speak. You might try taking a moment to think before you respond. Does that make sense to you?

your request to one or two specific actions. Don't be overbearing or dictatorial. Be responsive to the other person. Ask for feedback or agreement. Perhaps you will need to change your behavior in this situation, too.

When you are specific about the change you want, you can monitor the other person's progress. If Carl does homework for only half an hour, instead of the hour you agreed on, tell him. If Lynn interrupts, tell her right on the spot. Simply give the information; don't get emotional or lecture.

✓ TRADEOFF

State what the other person is apt to gain by changing his or her behavior. Think carefully about what the other person wants, what will truly motivate him or her, keeping in mind that people are more apt to be motivated by reward than by punishment.

If you have spoken about this problem before and you think it is necessary to mention negative consequences, then do so, but try a TACTful message with positive consequences first. In all cases, avoid threats; they only lead to counterthreats and arguments.

Be very careful to avoid judgments and labels when stating your tradeoff (and, for that matter, in the other parts of a TACTful message). The more aware you are of those words and phrases, the less you will use them. Here are some commonly used ones: that's wrong, bad, boring, disrespectful, dumb, terrible, awful. Or, you are irresponsible, stupid, clumsy, disorganized, lazy, too sensitive, slow, conceited, loud, crazy.

Judgment words reflect opinions; when giving a TACTful message, stick to the facts.

AN EXERCISE IN WRITING TACTFUL MESSAGES

To prepare for writing your own TACTful message, start by editing one that was written by a manager in a workshop I conducted. This was Ernie's first TACTful message, and it needed editing. Ernie was not used to giving criticism this way; most of us aren't. Your own TACTful messages will probably need to be carefully edited, too, and this exercise is good preparation.

POOR	GOOD
If you don't shape up, your work will continue to suffer and so will your chances for promotion.	Your work has been good up till now. You'll be able to maintain your excellence and improve; that means a better job appraisal.
If you don't pay attention, I'll find someone else to do the job and you'll be up the creek without a paddle.	If you pay close attention you may find that that Project is more interesting and complicated than you thought. Your active participation will help your overall job performance and make you feel part of the team. I'm sure you'll feel good about that, and so will I.
If you don't listen to me, why should I listen to you?	If I have a sense you are really listening and trying to understand me, I will be motivated to listen to you. This should open up our communication and lead to deeper understanding.

When you have finished editing Ernie's message below, compare it with the rewritten model that follows. This is what Ernie wrote in his first try:

Who is involved? Walt, the shop foreman.

Give a brief statement about the background of the problem: Walt constantly yells across the room to give assignments to his workers.

Tell the other person what his or her unwanted behavior is. Describe exactly what he or she has been doing.
"Walt, when you yell across the room to ask someone to do something, you are being insensitive about his feelings."

Affect. How does this behavior affect you, the relationship, or the organization? Use "I" statements and express your feelings about the behavior.
"I am concerned about this because different people have said you are being disrespectful."

Change. Request a specific change in the person's behavior.
"If you want someone to do something, please walk up to the person and tell him one-on-one."

Tradeoff. State what the other person is apt to gain by changing his or her behavior. (Or what he or she is apt to lose if previous attempts to point out the rewards of the change have not been successful.)
"I feel you will gain the respect of the people you supervise because you will not be turning them off with your disrespect for them as individuals."

Ernie's Tell phrase, "you are being insensitive about his feelings" is judgmental and should be omitted. A better TELL line would be: "Walt, you frequently yell across the room to ask someone to do something. You did that twice yesterday and three times on Wednesday."

Under Affect, Ernie had written, "Different people have said you are being disrespectful." But it is better to speak for yourself, not others. Also, the word "disrespectful" is judgmental. How does Ernie know if Walt is being disrespectful? He could just be loud. An improved Affect line would be: "I am concerned about this because it interrupts the orderly flow of work."

Ernie's request for Change—"If you want someone to do something, please walk up to the person and tell him one-on-one."—was specific and direct. Well done!

His Tradeoff, though, is extremely judgmental. Respect and disrespect are loaded words, as is Ernie's phrase "turning them off." The more you practice giving TACTful messages, the more attuned you will become to words that are judgmental. The Tradeoff line could read: "I believe that if you go up and speak to people one-on-one, they are more apt to listen to what you are saying and give you a good response.

PREPARING YOUR OWN TACTFUL MESSAGE

Using the format below, write a TACTful message that will help resolve a problem you are having. You may want to start with something that is of little consequence to you and write, edit, and deliver a few practice messages before addressing a serious business situation or a problem in an intimate relationship.

If, however, you have been following the guidelines and practicing the exercises in this book, you are probably prepared to give a TACTful message to almost anyone.

Giving a TACTful message is the next logical step beyond stating a position. When you state a position, you have observed and listened, you are objective, you have thought about the problem. Now you move on to requesting the other person's participation in solving the problem.

When you write your TACTful message, use the first person. Write down exactly what you would say to the other person in a face-to-face encounter. If you make a number of copies of the blank message format, you will always have one handy when you need to prepare a TACTful message.

The TACTful Message

Who is involved? _____

Give a brief statement about the background of the problem:

_____

_____

_____

_____

Tell the other person what his or her unwanted behavior is. Describe exactly what he or she has been doing.

_____

_____

_____

_____

Affect. How does this behavior affect you, the relationship, or the organization? Use "I" statements and express your feelings about the behavior.

_____

_____

_____

_____

Change. Request a specific change in the other person's behavior.

_____

_____

_____

_____

Tradeoff. State what the other person is apt to gain by changing his or her behavior. (Or what he or she is apt to lose if previous attempts to point out the rewards of the change have not been successful.)

_____

_____

_____

_____

When you have written your message, check it by asking yourself the following questions:

1. Is the TELL line brief and specific? Does it clearly and objectively identify the problem? Or is my TELL line nothing more than a long list of grievances? (If it is, categorize your list and pick one or

two specific behaviors to concentrate on now. Return to other troublesome behaviors when you have made progress with the first ones you address.)

2. Have I described the other person's behavior objectively, or have I talked about attitudes, motives or intentions? Have I tried to be a mind-reader?

3. Have I made any judgments of the other person's behavior?

4. Have I taken responsibility for my feelings rather than blaming them on the other person? Have I said, "That makes me feel . . ." or "You make me feel . . ."?

5. Have I ridiculed, put down, or labeled the other person?

6. Have I been emotionally restrained or have I been dramatic?

7. Have I avoided old catch phrases the other person is used to hearing from me? Have I expressed myself in a new, positive way?

8. Have I proposed only one or two specific changes in behavior?

9. Have I asked the other person for a commitment to and/or a time-frame for change? Have I given him or her a chance to disagree with me?

10. Have I anticipated counterproposals or questions about the behavior change?

11. Have I stressed the rewards and positive consequences?

12. Are these rewards/consequences appropriate? Will the other person respond to them?

13. Can I realistically follow through and deliver these rewards/consequences?

14. If I have had to present negative consequences, am I prepared to follow through with them?

If you find during the editing process that you need to make changes, do not be discouraged. That's what the editing is for. With practice and experience you'll make fewer.

DELIVERING A SUCCESSFUL TACTFUL MESSAGE

When you have written and edited the message to your satisfaction, you are ready to deliver it. Here are a few pointers that will encourage success.

1. *Wait for your feelings and thoughts to be in balance before giving criticism.* Don't deliver a criticism when you are hot under the collar. Wait until you have had time to vent, observe, objectify, think, and prepare a TACTful message.

2. *Know your intent.* Before giving a criticism, ask yourself honestly, am I trying to improve performance or help someone grow? Or do I just want to have things done my way or to prove that I'm right? If your criticism does not have positive intent, don't give it. A TACTful message must have positive intent.

3. *Know your desired outcome.* Ask yourself, What do I want to happen? Do I want to find the best solution to the problem? Do I want to help the other person change? Or do I want to get rid of some uncomfortable feelings? Or one-up the other person? If your desired outcome will improve the situation or relationship, go ahead with your criticism. If your desired outcome is self-serving, wait and think again about your intent.

4. *Ask the other person to take time to think about the criticism before responding.* This can be a highly effective tactic. It will enhance listening because the other person will feel less pressured and will be less likely to think about a response while you are talking.

5. *Be prepared for a variety of responses.* From your knowledge of the other person, you may be able to anticipate his or her response, but be prepared for surprises. Listen carefully and think about every response you get to a criticism, whether or not it is the one you anticipated. Take as much time as you need —a minute or a day—before responding.

6. *Remain open.* Pascal wrote, "When we wish to correct with advantage, and show another that he errs, we must notice from what side he views the matter, for on that side it is usually true, and admit the truth to him, but reveal to him the side on which it is false." Remaining open to whatever response you get will help you understand the other person's point of view. You can show him or her what, as Pascal says, is true or false only after you know the way he or she views the situation.

   If your partner becomes highly emotional or attacks you, then you should suggest that you both back off for a while and think things over. You will never understand the other person's point of view if he or she cannot state it rationally. Be careful not to accuse the person of being out of control, childish, or spiteful. Make a simple, unemotional statement that it is time to take a break.

7. *Prepare yourself.* Initially, you will want to write out your TACTful messages. As you become more comfortable with the technique, you will have to do this less and less, or only on occasions when there is a lot at stake. After writing out your TACTful message, rehearse it aloud. If you are very nervous, ask a friend to listen to your message and give you feedback. Or role play, asking your friend to take the part of the person to whom you will deliver the message. Role-playing prepares you to anticipate questions, defenses, or counterattacks.

As you practice, envision yourself delivering the message. See yourself remaining calm and confident. Hear your steady, confident voice. Use affirmations such as:

"Giving criticism is much easier if I am prepared. I am prepared."

"I am criticizing John to improve our relationship/improve his performance/contribute to his personal growth."

"Giving thoughtful, well-prepared feedback is a way of being open and honest. I am recognizing a problem and stating my position on it."

"Giving honest feedback leads to greater intimacy."

"I deliver this criticism carefully and confidently."

Anticipate the pride and sense of accomplishment you will have when you have delivered your TACTful message. Congratulate yourself for giving a thoughtful, careful message.

If you suspect the other person will interrupt a face-to-face delivery of a TACTful message to the point where you will not be able to complete it, then write it. You may also wish to deliver your message in writing if you believe the other person's listening skills are so poor that your message will fall on deaf ears. Writing a message is not a guarantee that it will be understood or attended to, but it does give the other person the opportunity to think about and re-read it as many times as necessary for clarification.

WHAT A TACTFUL MESSAGE DOES FOR YOU

A TACTful message clarifies in your own mind exactly what the problem is. You may find when you write out your message that the problem is quite different from what you originally thought.

A TACTful message helps you to articulate and be aware of your feelings. Since feelings motivate so much of our behavior, it is a good idea to know what they are. We are then less likely to be unknowingly controlled by them.

The TACTful message forces you to think in terms of behavior instead of judging and labeling others when you criticize them. It takes some effort to get used to this way of thinking. If someone shouts a lot, we tend to label him or her as rude. That isn't necessarily true. The only thing that is objectively true is that the person shouts.

Judgments and labels invite defensiveness, denials, counterattacks, or withdrawals; they also can have a reinforcing effect. If you continually tell someone that he or she is clumsy, lazy, ungrateful, you are reinforcing the behavior that causes you to label the person that way.

TACTful messages enable you to express what you want from the other person in specific, unambiguous terms. They also help you think positively. Most of us are used to thinking in terms of negative consequences of behavior, not positive consequences. Negative consequences, however, frequently cause unrest and rebellion. By focusing on the positive in tradeoffs, you offer a much stronger motivation for cooperation.

The TACTful message model gets results because it eliminates words and phrases that can get recipients defensive, angry, or hurt. They are more likely to listen and less likely to counterattack or become highly emotional.

The TACTful message is active, not reactive. You have taken the initiative to describe and seek a solution to a problem. Because you have objectified and thought about the problem, you can remain calm and unprovoked when you state your position.

In the workplace, writing out your TACTful message, even after you have become comfortable with the technique, gives you a record of what you have said to an employee about his or her job performance. If an employee later accuses you of unfair treatment, a written record of what was said and the number of times it was said is helpful.

For two years, Ed had been working directly under the vice-president of a major corporation. Ed liked and respected his boss, Alan, but there was one problem that triggered a great deal of anger and frustration for Ed. Alan scheduled, rescheduled, and cancelled meetings at a moment's notice by having his secretary call Ed's secretary. He rarely checked with Ed to see if Ed could manage the change. Ed felt bypassed and belittled by Alan's treatment.

Ed wanted to deliver a TACTful message but was not sure he could. After all, Alan was a busy, important vice-president. With the encouragement and support of the workshop group, Ed decided to deliver his message during the lunch break. When Ed returned from lunch, he was beaming.

This is the message he delivered:

TELL: "Just this morning, you rescheduled a meeting we were to have at the end of the day. Since I have been working for you, you've been changing meeting times at a moment's notice. For instance, you cancelled or rescheduled four times this week. On each of those occasions, your secretary called to tell my secretary."

AFFECT: "I feel angry, frustrated, and bypassed. Frustrated because I have to reschedule things that are important to me and it is often difficult for me to juggle my appointments. Bypassed because I don't hear from you personally."

CHANGE: "I would appreciate it if you thought carefully before rescheduling and examined whether a change is absolutely necessary. It would be nice if you could call me yourself sometimes to see how we can best arrange our appointments."

TRADEOFF: "I think I'll be able to use my time more efficiently if I don't have to reschedule so often. And I'll probably feel better about our working relationship, because admittedly, I have built up some anger and frustration over this issue."

Alan responded to Ed's message by saying, "Why didn't you bring this up sooner? You've been working for me for two years. I never knew this was a problem for you."

Eight months later I ran into Ed. "The TACTful message really worked," he reported with delight. "Alan doesn't reschedule meetings nearly so often now, and he frequently calls me personally to make the changes. I think he respects me more, and I certainly have a great deal more self-respect."

WHAT A TACTFUL MESSAGE WILL NOT DO FOR YOU

A TACTful message ensures the best delivery but does not mean that the other person will accommodate you; it will not get you your own way, either immediately or at any time in the future. Sometimes it takes a while for a recipient to really hear your message, and you may get what you want when you have repeated your message several times. There are, however, no guarantees.

Nor will a TACTful message change the other person. The other person may change some of his or her behavior patterns but will still be the same person. Don't get caught in the trap of trying to change someone's personality. The most you can do is solicit cooperation in changing the specific behavior that adversely affects you or the relationship.

WHEN TO USE A TACTFUL MESSAGE

Determining who "owns" a problem will tell you when a TACTful message is or isn't in order. There are three possibilities here—the other person owns the problem, there is no problem, or you own the problem.

If the other person owns the problem, he or she will have the strong feelings, perhaps be confused or upset. In that case, you will want to call on a responsive skill— careful and/or reflective listening to help him or her work out the problem.

If there is no problem, keep it that way with a healthy dose of praise. Don't take moments of bliss or tranquillity for granted. Praise rewards and reinforces behavior that is desirable and acceptable. If things are going well, say so.

If you own the problem, you will know because you have the strong feelings. Something about another person's behavior has upset you. Since it is your problem, you will want to construct and deliver a TACTful message. Do this when your discontent with someone else's behavior has been building up over a period of time and is affecting your relationship or job performance, or when you have noticed a pattern of unwanted behavior and anticipate that the unwanted behavior will continue.

In the workplace, don't wait for a semi-annual review to tell an employee he or she is slipping. Ongoing feedback through a TACTful message will help get the employee back on the track.

You may have to deliver a message several times to break an established pattern of behavior. You need not repeat the entire TACTful message. Often, restating the CHANGE line in a more positive way will be enough. For example, "I know that you can be more demonstrative and animated in your presentations," or, "I'm sure you can keep up-to-date on these invoices." Encouraging positive behavior is the best way to get people to change.

WHEN A TACTFUL MESSAGE DOES NOT WORK

If you have given a message with a positive tradeoff a number of times and the person still exhibits the unwanted behavior, you may redeliver the message with a negative tradeoff. If you choose to do this, be very sure that you can or are willing to follow through on the negative consequences.

If you do not follow through on the negative consequences, you have made an idle threat, and an idle threat is a way of manipulating another person. Besides, how can the other person take you seriously if he or she knows you will not live up to your word?

There are situations where the negative consequences will be dire: leaving a job or relationship or firing an employee. Before delivering a message with extreme negative consequences, ask yourself, "Have I done all that I can do to adjust and accommodate in this situation?" If the answer is yes and you deliver the message, then it is crucial to remain silent and listen carefully to the other person's response. This is your last chance for open, honest communication, so you must do everything in your power to encourage discussion.

If the recipient counterattacks or tries to manipulate or circumvent you, urge him or her to take some time to think about what you've said and talk again later. If you still cannot arrive at a workable solution or salvage the relationship, then at least you will know that you have done as much as was humanly possible in the circumstances. Leaving the job or relationship or firing the employee may not be easy, but your sincere efforts will have shown you that you have no other options in the situation. Of course, you will have other opportunities outside the job or relationship, and you would do well for yourself to explore them before delivering a message with extreme negative consequences.

CASE HISTORIES

Here are a series of TACTful messages that were used in the case histories we have been following.

✓ DOMINATE / CONTROL

Anna delivered her TACTful message to George when she was fully prepared and when George was not in the midst of one of his lectures to her. She asked that he stay quiet and listen until she had finished speaking and that he take anywhere from an hour to a day to respond to her. Since George was accustomed to interrupting her to argue, this tactic was effective in allowing Anna to say her full piece. Even though there were a number of times that she faltered, forgot, or simply ran out of energy, she could report measurable success. Over time, their communication and intimacy improved.

Tell: "George, you don't let up on your suggestions about how I ought to behave or lead my life. Three times this week you have told me what I should or shouldn't do about participating in an aerobics class and adult education classes."

Affect: "I'm tired of your telling me how to conduct my affairs. I am also concerned that if I allow this to continue, it will whittle away my self-esteem. I won't let that happen again."

Change: "Please stop telling me what to do. If you have a suggestion and I disagree, then leave the topic alone."

Tradeoff: "I believe that our relationship will be strengthened, and you will have less to take care of. You will be able to relax and focus on your own problems when you leave mine up to me."

✓ *MANIPULATE*

This is what Tom finally said to Jenny on the subject of calling him at his office:

Tell: "Mother, you frequently call me at the office to tell me that I don't call you enough. You talk about other sons who you think demonstrate more love to their mothers than I do."

Affect: "When you do this, at first I feel angry, and then put off and sad. Put off because it's hard to talk to you, and this makes me want to avoid it. Sad because I am afraid this problem will permanently damage our relationship."

Change: "I would like you to stop phoning me at the office and making remarks that imply I don't care about you. I would also like you to try to enjoy the time we do have together instead of dwelling on the time we don't have together."

Tradeoff: "I think doing this will strengthen our relationship. I will want to talk to you more if we can talk about things that are pleasant to both of us."

✓ *PUNISH / GET EVEN*

Mary continued occasionally to punish Bill in public. He had built up some resentment and decided to deliver a TACTful message to ask Mary to discontinue her punishing behavior.

Tell: "Two days ago, Mary, when we were having dinner with Dick and Ellen, you said that I'm never home. You have publicly complained about my heavy workload on other recent occasions."

Affect: "I resent your public remarks about this. I thought that from our previous conversations we both realized that I have to devote a great deal of time to my work at this point in my career."

Change: "I would appreciate it if you would stop complaining in public. Let's talk about this issue again, just the two of us, and try to reach a resolution. I don't want you to continue to bring it up in public."

Tradeoff: "I think this will strengthen our relationship. If I allow resentment to build, it will come between us. When an issue is not resolved, being open and honest about our feelings will help us resolve it. This too will strengthen our relationship."

✓ *ABUSE*

After extensive individual counseling, group work, and careful thought, Margaret decided there were certain things she just did not want to live with. If Bob's public ridicule, name-calling, and venomous outbursts continued, she was prepared to leave the relationship. There was not enough loving support to warrant staying.

Tell: "Bob, over the past two years you have continued to make sarcastic remarks and put-downs at my expense, both publicly and privately. You did that just last night and now again this morning."

Affect: "I feel confused because I have told you many times that I can't bear this. You are supposed to love me, yet you continue to treat me this way. And I feel sad because I feel our marriage is very troubled."

Change: "I would like you to stop making derogatory remarks about me in front of other people and when we're alone. I would also like you to listen to what I have to say without telling me I am 'too sensitive' or 'insecure.'"

Tradeoff: "If you listened carefully and paid attention to what I say, you would understand that I cannot and will not compromise on this. I do not intend to continue in a relationship in which I am the target of ongoing put-downs, sarcasm, and ridicule."

Bob's listening skills never improved to the point where he could hear what Margaret was saying to him. He continued to ridicule her publicly and privately. Having done as much as she could to salvage the relationship, Margaret left Bob.

✓ *SLICE*

Cynthia was finally up to her eyebrows with Stan's slicing and so she delivered a TACTful message.

Tell: "You frequently say things to me like, 'You're too sensitive,' or 'You're stupid.'"

Affect: "I feel hurt and angry when you say things like that."

Change: "Please stop making cutting remarks to me."

Tradeoff: "If you don't say things like that, our relationship will improve and we'll be able to get our joint assignments done more quickly and efficiently."

✓ *GET ATTENTION*

After Herb continued to interrupt at meetings, Jonathan devised this message:

Tell: "You frequently break into my presentations with remarks like, 'You haven't had enough time to re-

search this thoroughly.' You did that just this morning."

Affect: "I am concerned about this because it stops the
flow of our meetings and wastes time."

Change: "If you have questions or comments, please
hold them until I've finished my presentation."

Tradeoff: "Our meetings will finish sooner and the work
will go more smoothly for everyone."

✓   CHANGE YOU

Tony used a TACTful message to make a last-ditch
effort to get Jane to stop trying to change him.

Tell: "Jane, since we were married you have asked me to
change several basic things about myself, such as the
type of clothes I wear and the way I conduct myself at
parties."

Affect: "I feel confused and hurt when you do this. Confused because I thought you knew who and what I
was before we got married, and hurt because it seems
as though you are looking for a man who is different
from me."

Change: "I would like you to stop trying to remake me."

Tradeoff: "If you can accept me for what I am, you
might feel more relaxed and our relationship would
improve. I am willing to change some aspects of my
behavior, but I cannot and will not become someone
else."

✓   GET YOU OFF THE TRACK

Despite defusing, genuine inquiry, and stating his position, Jim was still having a hard time with Steve. He
delivered this TACTful message to try to resolve the situation:

Tell: "Steve, when I talk to you about your work, you
often interrupt by saying things like, 'You're giving

me a hard time now that you're manager,' or 'Why are
you singling me out?'"

Affect: "I feel frustrated when you do this because I am
trying to point out ways for you to improve your performance."

Change: "When I talk to you about your work, I would
like you to listen carefully and think about what I
say."

Tradeoff: "If you really pay attention to my observations
it could help you improve your performance and increase your chances for promotion."

✓ *UNDERMINE*

Rita used the following message to smoke out Sally
and strip her of her camouflage:

Tell: "Sally, you frequently make remarks under your
breath or gesture when I'm talking at meetings. This
morning you put your thumbs down while I was
speaking. Also, three or four staff members have
mentioned that you have made negative comments
about me to them."

Affect: "I'm concerned that this kind of behavior undermines our working relationship and our ability to get
things done together."

Change: "If you disagree with any of my decisions or
proposals please say so openly in meetings or talk to
me directly."

Tradeoff: "This will enable both of us to be direct with
each other and give us a chance to work out our differences. And it will improve the general office atmosphere."

Sally listened with apparent unconcern and then said,
"Rita, honey, I just don't know what you're talking
about. You're imagining things."

"I'm not imagining it, Sally. I saw you whisper and
gesture, and three or four people have told me that you

have talked about me behind my back." Rita continued
to state her position, using the broken record technique.
She did not waste time or breath, defending herself to
Sally, but calmly repeated her CHANGE line. (It's not
necessary to use the exact words, as long as you do not
change the facts.)

"You're just too sensitive for words, Rita."

"I would like you to talk to me openly and directly
whenever you disagree with a decision or proposal I've
made."

Although she did not get Sally to agree to the change
requested in her message, Rita took the adult position by
bringing the problem out into the open.

✓   GET ONE'S OWN WAY

Sarah chose times when Larry was calm to deliver her
TACTful message about "peace and quiet."

Tell: "Larry, the other evening when the children had
    friends over, you stormed into the family room and
    told them their friends had to leave within half an
    hour so you could get to sleep."
Affect: "I feel angry and disgusted when this happens
    because I think the kids have a right to have their
    friends in and enjoy themselves from time to time."
Change: "I would like you to stop and think before
    reacting so quickly when other people in the house-
    hold are making noise or disrupting what you consider
    to be 'peace.' Please take time to think before you
    rush in and start shouting."
Tradeoff: "If you take time to collect your thoughts, per-
    haps you won't react so quickly and so vehemently.
    Taking time to think about what is fair for everyone
    could enrich your relationship with the children and
    with me."

✓   GET A LAUGH

A TACTful message is an effective preventive measure where toxic humor is concerned.

Tell: "You frequently try to get a laugh at someone else's expense. Just yesterday you commented on Howie's 'crazy ideas.'"

Affect: "I feel turned off by that kind of joke. I don't like it, and I don't respect it."

Change: "Why don't you try to get a laugh by using more positive humor instead of using sarcasm or put-downs?"

Tradeoff: "I'd enjoy being around you much more if you dropped sarcasm from your repertoire. I think if you did, a lot more people would realize how funny and talented you are."

SOME FINAL POINTERS:

Reserve your TACTful message for those moments of calm when both you and your partner are ready to exchange thoughts, opinions, and feelings.

The reason for delivering a TACTful message is to discuss your dislike of someone else's behavior. It sometimes is helpful to mention a positive attribute as well. For example, Sarah could have prefaced her message to Larry with, "Larry, you have always been a generous, caring husband and father. But..." You might choose this approach if you are dealing with an extremely sensitive person. Just remember that if you always praise first and mention the problem second, the recipient will come to associate criticism with praise. To avoid that trap it is often better to offer praise when things are running smoothly and deliver a TACTful message to get things back on the track when they're not.

The other person may not be ready to hear, understand, or respond to your message. People develop various mechanisms for blocking out what they are not ready to deal with. Sensing that someone is not ready to hear a message does not mean you don't send it. To remain in the adult position and express your feelings constructively, you may have to get a problem out in the open. You will save yourself frustration and disappointment, however, if you are aware that the other person may not be able to respond. Don't let the other person's possible unresponsiveness stop you from sending your message, though. Holding back your honest emotions can put your mental and physical health at risk.

Ideally, the recipient has an interest in your feelings and in minimizing your discomfort. In that case, both the Affect and the Tradeoff motivate the recipient to change. This, however, is not always true. When you realize that the other person is not interested in your feelings, or in situations where your feelings are simply beside the point, you must rely on the Tradeoff as your sole motivator. In these cases, you will want to up the ante to better motivate change, taking into account what the other person really wants.

The TACTful message provides a helpful and effective model for delivering constructive criticism. It allows us to confront situations we might otherwise avoid as unpleasant, anxiety-producing, or too time-consuming. Because it forces us to be objective, we can give constructive criticism without giving offense. This objectivity encourages you to deliver only well-intended criticism. Using the TACTful message model precludes irrational attacks or needless venting of feelings on those whose behavior adversely affects us.

For the recipient, the TACTful message takes the pain out of receiving a criticism. A recipient is much more likely to listen to, think about, and respond favorably to an objective and calmly delivered criticism. With the proper motivation, the recipient can change specific aspects of his or her behavior, whereas it is virtually impossible for anyone to respond positively to a string of subjective judgments and sweeping generalizations.

The TACTful message brings your skills for coping with criticism full circle. You know how to take criticism well, and you know how to give it well, too. When you stop to think about it, the skills on both sides are much the same. To give criticism well, you must silently observe and listen carefully, objectify and distance yourself, ask questions to clarify the problem, and be able to state and maintain your position. These are the same skills that enable you to take criticism well.

Now you can take criticism without letting it damage your self-esteem, and you can give criticism without damaging anyone else's self-esteem. You can criticize others in the same calm, controlled, adult manner in which you would wish to be criticized. In your life, and in the lives of those around you, criticism can at last take its rightful place as your best tool for growth, improvement, and fulfillment.

INDEX

215

About the Author

MARY LYNNE HELDMANN is president of her own consulting firm, Heldmann Associates, and conducts skills training programs for school districts, colleges, hospitals, corporations, government agencies, and community groups. Ms. Heldmann was formerly a Family Counselor.

Mary Lynne lives with her husband and three sons in Glens Falls, New York.

EMPOWERMENT

THROUGH

EDUCATION

AND SELF-HELP